THE HOMESTEAD WINTER PANTRY

GEORGIA VAROZZA

TEN PEAKS PRESS®
EUGENE, OR

Cover and interior design by Dugan Design Group
Photography by Jay Eads

For bulk or special sales, please call 1 (800) 547-8979.
Email: CustomerService@hhpbooks.com

Neither the author nor publisher is responsible for any outcome from use of this cookbook. The recipes are intended for informational purposes and those who have the appropriate culinary skills. USDA guidelines should always be followed in food preparation and canning. The author and publisher make no warranty, express or implied, in any recipe.

 TEN PEAKS PRESS is a federally registered trademark of The Hawkins Children's LLC.
Harvest House Publishers, Inc., is the exclusive licensee of this trademark.

THE HOMESTEAD WINTER PANTRY

Copyright © 2025 by Georgia Varozza
Published by Ten Peaks Press, an imprint of Harvest House Publishers
Eugene, Oregon 97408

ISBN 978-0-7369-9069-1 (pbk)
ISBN 978-0-7369-9070-7 (eBook)

Library of Congress Control Number: 2024947437

Printed in China

25 26 27 28 29 30 / DC / 10 9 8 7 6 5 4 3 2 1

For Matthew—
You loosed the surly bonds of earth far too soon. I miss you.

For Paula—
Thank you for all your help.
It's cliché, but I couldn't have done it without you!

For Walker and Sara—
Your goodness to me is so appreciated.
I love you guys!

CONTENTS

INTRODUCTION

WHY A WINTER PANTRY?

When summer is upon us and the days are warm, it might be difficult to contemplate winter weather, but that's exactly when we should be thinking about such things. A bit of organizing and preparing now can save us worries in the future when a quick trip to the store for necessities might be impossible, so having the ability to "shop" at home makes good sense.

I continually maintain a storage of food supplies, water, nonelectric light, and a method to cook and heat that isn't tied to the power grid. I try to keep my vehicle at least half full of gas, and I make sure to put away extra food for my animals. We live in the country, and we are just about guaranteed to lose our power several times throughout the year, so being prepared is a way of life for us.

It's January as I'm writing this. If you could look outside my window, you'd see nothing but white—the result of a snowstorm immediately followed by an ice storm. For three days now, we have been forced to stay home because the roads are a deadly sheet of ice, and the forecast is calling for another ice storm to hit by tomorrow morning. The power is out. Schools and stores are closed, and there are no plans yet for anything to open in the next day or two. The only sounds we hear are the crack of tree limbs breaking (and sometimes whole trees by the sounds of it) under the weight of the ice. Keeping ourselves warm, our bodies fueled, and our livestock and pets fed and watered is a treacherous job.

This area has been my home for forty years, and I've never seen the weather bring us to such an abrupt and lengthy halt. It's weirdly serendipitous that I'm experiencing such an extraordinary weather event at the same time I'm writing a book about stocking your winter pantry. Thankfully, we're prepared.

The title of this book is *The Homestead Winter Pantry*, but the need for a stash of necessities can happen anytime and isn't necessarily weather related. My aim here isn't to write a "prepper" type tome, but rather a commonsense, easy-to-implement book that helps families think about the what ifs and confidently navigate unexpected disruptions to daily living. Do a bit of research to ascertain what risks are associated with your area and plan accordingly, but here is a list to help you start thinking about potential hazards:

- Weather—blizzards, flooding, hurricanes, etc.
- Power outages
- Wildfires
- Recession or loss of employment
- Earthquakes and tsunamis
- Chain-of-supply disruptions and transportation difficulties
- Pandemics
- Social unrest and riots
- Solar flares

Planning for our winter needs will provide confidence and peace because we'll know we can feed and care for our families when uncertain times hit. I know that's true for my family. And because we *are* prepared, we are getting through this current ice storm in relative comfort. Yes, it's quite a change from our normal routine, but we're making the best of the situation.

How the Book Is Organized

The first part of the book will concentrate on the big picture and how to prepare for emergencies. Hopefully, it will bring awareness to any gaps in your ability to stay safe and carry on when misfortune hits.

The second part of the book will be the fun part—pantry essentials, bulk mixes, tasty recipes that take advantage of the season (and take advantage of our pantries that we've organized and filled with good things!), and a resource page to help you find the food and tools that will make life easier.

My hope is that you gain a clearer perspective on how to become a bit more self-reliant should disaster come knocking on your door…or even if it's just a wee detour from your daily schedule. It's nice to be prepared!

PART ONE

THE BIG PICTURE

Day-to-day living keeps us busy. We work, take care of our loved ones, stay in touch with friends and family, maintain our homes and possessions, and pursue our interests and hobbies. We pay bills, go to the doctor, and worry about our jobs and taxes. At the end of most days we fall, exhausted, into bed, sleep less than we should, and then get up and do it all over again. There's just so much to do!

So why on earth would we voluntarily choose to add more to the mix by planning and preparing for lean times or emergencies? For me, the answer is easy: I love knowing that my family can navigate the unexpected and will be just fine. And even more, I love having an active hand in those preps. I garden, can, and dehydrate the produce, I buy meat and poultry in bulk to pressure can and freeze, and I keep chickens for eggs. It's a good life.

Over the years, I've given thought to what's important in life, and my answer varies depending on what I'm currently experiencing. But when I contemplate emergency situations, I hone in on the basics: heat, light, shelter, water, and food.

Now, since this is a book titled *The Homestead Winter Pantry*, I'll focus on what we need to store to comfortably see our families through a winter without the need to leave the home, and I'll offer up tasty recipes that will take advantage of the season.

But first, let's touch on those basics—heat, light, shelter, water, and food—because when an emergency hits, you don't want to be caught unaware. Hopefully, thinking about these basics will get you started on the road to wintertime (or anytime) self-reliance.

One last thing: Keep a notebook handy while you read, and jot down anything that you'd like to pursue. With this convenient list, you'll be able to budget items that you think will be useful given your particular circumstances.

HEAT AND LIGHT

W e need some way to stay warm, have light, and cook our food. It's all fine until the power goes out, isn't it? Suddenly, you're without the ability to prepare a hot meal or keep warm. But a bit of foresight and preparation will see you through. Here are some possibilities:

Heat

Obviously, if you have a generator, you'll hardly notice that the power is out. Make sure it has been properly installed and serviced and is ready to go well before winter sets in. Don't bring the generator indoors, and remember to have fuel to run it.

Here at the Varozza homestead, we use wood for heat (and for cooking when the power is off!). We go through a lot of wood, so we make sure to have about three cords of seasoned wood on hand at the beginning of winter. It's always smart to fill your woodpile before you need it.

And of course, there's solar heat and natural gas.

But what do you do if you're part of the 40 percent of people whose only source of heat comes from the power grid? You'll need some backup during an outage. First, wear layers. Layering clothing provides more warmth than wearing one thick layer. Top the layers with a heavy sweater, coat, or blanket. Clothing comprised of wool or silk will be more effective than most types of synthetics.

Keep everyone in one room with the door closed. Close your blinds and curtains, and cover doors and windows with blankets or clothing. Cover heating vents and pay special attention to any places where cold air can sneak inside. If the sun is out, you can open the curtains on south-facing windows to take advantage of solar gain. Just be sure it's making a warming difference in the house. If you have a tent, bring it inside and have the family sleep together to help retain body heat.

You can also purchase portable propane heaters that are safe to use indoors. I tried a popular brand and found that the initial cost wasn't prohibitive, but the cost of the propane canisters added up in a hurry. Still, during really cold weather, these types of heaters are useful. Even though they are rated as safe to use indoors, place the heater near a window that has been slightly cracked open when using.

If you have a way to heat water, fill a hot water bottle and place it on your stomach; be careful that you don't accidentally burn your skin. Most of our heat loss is through the skin that's exposed to the elements, so it makes sense to cover yourself completely. Wear socks, gloves or mittens, and a hat or scarf you can wrap around your head.

Maybe some of you have read about or heard of a DIY mini heater that pairs a terra-cotta flowerpot with a smaller flowerpot saucer? The saucer should be just big enough to hold about four tea lights, and the idea is that it can heat a very small area.

You place the saucer right side up on nonflammable material on the floor or other suitable surface. Next, stack one or two bricks (or some other fire-resistant block) on either side of the saucer so they are a bit higher than the top of the saucer sides. The goal is to invert the pot over the saucer, resting the inverted pot on the bricks with several inches of space between the top of the saucer sides and the bottom edge of the pot. Essentially, you've made a domed chamber. Add about four tea light candles to the saucer and light them. The heat moves up, and the inverted terra-cotta pot "catches" the heat to warm the immediate area.

I decided to experiment and found that while it did throw out heat, it wasn't much, and I needed to stay very close to the pot. It certainly didn't heat even the small room I was in, but it did eventually raise the temperature several degrees in the immediate area. I also watched it like a hawk because it was an open flame, which made me nervous, and I concluded that I wouldn't be comfortable using this around kids or pets. But I've read that some folks have used it under extreme circumstances such that they feared they would freeze to death otherwise. My suggestion? Figure out another alternate heat source before the need arises. (I added the information here because it keeps showing up online, and I wanted to give you fair warning if you're contemplating this.)

Cooking

Cooking during an outage might be problematic as well. If you have a barbeque grill or camp stove, you're set. Just make sure you have a good supply of propane or charcoal ready to go. You can also buy small emergency stoves that use canned fuel. I've seen them for sale for as low as ten dollars, so if the budget is tight, these are a great choice. Just keep in mind that these stoves are tiny, so you won't be cooking large amounts of food with them. But heating up a couple cans of soup or something similar is totally doable. I've used (with success) the Emergency Zone Fold Flat Aluminum Stove; it retails for closer to twenty-five dollars but comes with four fuel canisters. Again, you won't be cooking meals for a family with it, but you'll be able to take care of basic cooking needs.

Solar ovens are another great option, and they really do work (although not on cloudy or rainy days, alas). When I use a solar oven, I make sure to be available during the cooking process because as the sun moves through the sky I need to periodically turn the oven so it directly faces the sun at all times. This ensures that the oven stays hot enough to thoroughly cook the food.

If you're cooking for a family (although it will work for one or two folks just as easily), the All-American Sun Oven can't be beat. The Sun Oven can bake biscuits, bread, and cookies, roast a whole chicken or small turkey, cook stews, casseroles, and vegetables, pasteurize water, and reach temperatures of up to 400° on a clear day. There is a self-leveling rack inside that holds your cooking pots upright, so you don't have to worry about tipping.

Other popular solar ovens are GoSun portable ovens, the Haines 2.0 SunUp Solar Cooker and Dutch Oven, and the SolCook All Season Solar Cooker.

Light

I'm a devoted fan of lanterns and use them regularly. But during a power outage, their cachet rises considerably in my estimation. A couple of things to know:

High-quality lanterns work far better than the cheap ones you can get at most local stores, and they give off more light and less smoke. In fact, high-quality lanterns can shine as bright as an electric bulb. For years I used Aladdin lamps and loved them. But there was one issue for me—they hiss when lit. My son loves Aladdin lamps, and the noise doesn't bother him. He appreciates the bright light and the ease of locating spare parts. I ended up giving him my Aladdins and have switched to lanterns that are made in the French Alps. Because it's *not* easy to get replacement parts, I keep extras on hand and treat them with care. Keep in mind that inexpensive oil lanterns work just fine if you're simply wanting to stave off total darkness. I should also note that there are lanterns made specifically for outdoor use, as they don't blow out in breezy conditions. Dietz lanterns are great for barn work.

Quality lamp oil is a must. You can burn all sorts of oils in your lanterns including olive and palm kernel oils, but the mainstays are kerosene and paraffin because they are clean burning. Some lamp oils add scent, but unless you're planning on using your lanterns outside and want added citronella to keep mosquitoes at bay, stay away from those types. Same with colored oils, as they can stain your lantern over time. Whatever you use, keep your supply tightly covered (paraffin especially tends to evaporate) and in a safe place away from food, kids, and animals.

Candles are inexpensive, easily stored, and provide gentle light. Just make sure you have matches or lighters. The very cheapest candles have problems with smoke and soot buildup on the wicks, so spend an extra dollar or two and get decent candles. You'll be glad you did.

Flashlights are probably the most common alternate light source, but I confess that I don't have one because it seems the battery is dead whenever I need to use it and I scramble to find fresh batteries. But if flashlights are your go-to, always have a supply of extra batteries and you'll be fine.

2

WATER

I t's easy to overlook water in regard to emergencies because we tend to think of food first. But water is even more important to have than food. A person can't live more than three or four days or so without water, but we can go a month with no food if we have adequate water. If your water comes from a private well, the pump can't bring up the water if there's no power. But there are hand pumps that work without power (similar to what pioneers used long ago). They range from small emergency hand pumps to large systems that can be installed right along with your regular pump installation. A quick internet search will show you many different types to choose from.

Figuring your water needs isn't too difficult. The recommended amount to keep on hand is one gallon per person per day. About half of that should be used for drinking, and the other half for cooking, personal hygiene, and doing dishes or cleaning. Bear in mind that "daily water intake" can include broth, coffee or tea, and juice, so a gallon allotment per person per day might seem a bit extravagant. But let me just say, that gallon can go fast. For our family of seven, that equals seven gallons per day, and we try to stick to that number. If the forecast is calling for snow, ice, or heavy rain with flooding, we use the opportunity to collect emergency water. We set out very clean food-grade five-gallon buckets and large kitchen pots to catch the precipitation. Once filled, we bring the containers of snow inside to melt. We cover the containers and store some in a bathroom and some on an enclosed porch. We bring the containers inside when we need them and use this water for anything that doesn't require potable water—like flushing toilets. Store enough water so you can also use it for personal hygiene and cleaning. We stock paper plates, cups, and plastic silverware so we don't have to wash dishes, saving on our water usage. Under normal circumstances, disposable product usage goes against our mindset, but some years ago we learned the hard way that it's better to have paper goods than use precious water to clean dishes.

We also have horses, goats, chickens, dogs, and cats, so we keep a couple of large water troughs filled with water. And if the weather forecast calls for a big storm, we always fill up more troughs and five-gallon buckets. We cover the filled containers with weighted plywood so nothing gets in, and we use buckets to dip out water and take it to the livestock.

We also live near a good water source, and some years ago, I invested in a water purifying system. It's low tech and the filters need to be replaced occasionally. I make sure to always have extra filters. I also use our collected rainwater to pour into the water purifier when need be, which isn't very often because I maintain our potable water supply with dedication.

Sources for Emergency Water Collection

This list will help you think outside the box when it comes to accessing water in an emergency:

- ❏ Rainwater (don't collect rainwater from your roof, as it carries toxins; rather, collect into clean containers directly as the rain falls)
- ❏ Melted snow
- ❏ Toilet tank
- ❏ Water heater
- ❏ Household water pipes (even when the water is shut off, you can turn on the lowest faucet in your house and gravity will move the water through the pipes)
- ❏ Streams and other bodies of flowing water
- ❏ Natural springs

How to Make Water Safe in an Emergency

If you don't have a stockpile of clean water during an emergency, there are ways to get around the problem.

It *is* possible to make a DIY water filter. But like everything else, a bit of forethought and budgeting to purchase a filter or bottled water is far easier than adding another project to your to-do list. And to my way of thinking, water is the number one item to stock up on, because you won't last long without it. So it makes good sense to invest in a good filtering system. But what is a good filtering system? Ideally, you'll want something that provides enough filtered water each day for the number of people in your immediate care. That type of system is easy to find, but the cost goes up with the size of your filtering system.

For a do-it-yourself water filter, first collect the water you plan to filter (see the list above for collection ideas). Let the water sit undisturbed, so the bits of debris have a chance to settle (and be careful not to disturb that debris when it's time to filter). You'll first want to remove dirt, silt, sand, and sediment from your water: Once the water has settled, the first line of filtering defense is to pour the water through a double layer of coffee filters into a catch basin of some type.

Gather filter materials, such as activated charcoal, gravel, coarse sand, and cotton balls (the more types of materials you collect, the better the result). You'll also need a couple of two-liter plastic soda bottles or gallon water containers. These containers need tops that are funnel shaped, and at least one of them needs a cap you can screw on. Clean and sanitize the containers. Cut the bottoms off both containers.

Fill one of the containers with the filter material; begin by adding cotton balls to the funnel end and, moving upward, layer coarse sand, gravel, and finish with activated charcoal in the wide cut end. Tamp down lightly—the idea is that when you pour the water into this container, it will filter slowly.

Next, place the filter container (with screw top off) into the cut bottom of the second container so the funnel rests inside it a bit. When you are filtering water, you can unscrew the cap of the receiving container, so the clean water goes into a sanitized catch basin.

Now, is your water ready to use? Not quite! Boiling water is the best way to kill disease-causing organisms, including any remaining bacteria, parasites, and viruses. Bring the filtered water to a *full rolling boil* for one minute if you live between sea level and 1,000 feet in elevation. Boil two minutes up to 3,000 feet in elevation, three minutes up to 4,000 feet in elevation, and so on, up to six minutes.

This is a laborious, time-consuming way to get clean water, so my suggestion is to do what we do: Keep as many gallons of water as you can, stored in a dark outbuilding that doesn't freeze, and rotate your water regularly.

Adding Bleach for Long-Term Storage

Many folks buy one-gallon or five-gallon containers manufactured especially for storing water and fill them up with their household water. If you want to go this route, make sure the containers have been thoroughly cleaned before adding water. Then add liquid unscented bleach (make sure to use bleach strength of 4% to 5% sodium hypochlorite) as follows:

- Add 4 to 5 drops for a one-gallon container.
- Add 1 teaspoon bleach for a five-gallon container.

PART TWO

PANTRY ESSENTIALS

When you're unable to get to a store and all your meals must be made at home, a well-stocked pantry becomes essential. As you can imagine, there are many ingredients to have on hand if you're going to sail through emergencies in comfort. Also, the number of folks that you're preparing for can vary widely. You might live alone, with a spouse, or—like me—your food storage plan includes enough to feed seven people during a power outage or other disaster. As you go through the following list of pantry essentials, do your best to estimate how much of each you'll need based on the number of people you plan to feed. Write your list of essential items on paper and take that list with you to the store. As your budget allows, buy what you need, and mark it off your list.

FOOD STORAGE BASICS

Do your family a favor and add water to the top of your shopping list. As I mentioned in chapter 2, water is the most overlooked essential. Once you have your emergency water system worked out, you can turn your attention to food.

For years I've made a practice of having the ability to feed my family and friends for many months if the need arises. People often tease me and say that in the event of a disaster, they're all coming to my house! I must say, that makes me happy to know that I could indeed feed my family and friends for a very long while, and I'd gladly do so. I'm not suggesting that you must do the same, but I will say that a bit of advance preparation can make such a difference in how you face an emergency. The peace of mind in knowing your family will emerge from the storm unscathed can't be beat.

Gardening

Don't forget the benefits of gardening as part of your food storage plan. Some locations are warm enough to grow vegetables year-round, but for most of us, that's not the case. Still, there's a lot we can do to make our gardens productive longer each season and grow veggies that are known to be long keepers. Greenhouses and cold frames will extend the harvest season, and root cellars will hold veggies well into the deep part of winter. Don't have a root cellar? There are ways to get around that potential limitation with alternate storage options.

An unheated garage or basement is great if it is a cool, dark, and relatively moisture-free area. The most common root vegetables for storing all winter include hard-skinned winter squash, potatoes, sweet potatoes, carrots, onions, shallots, garlic, beets, turnips, and rutabagas. Carefully examine the vegetables you plan to save. You don't want any blemishes to mar the skin, because those are the places where contaminants can sneak in and spoil the veggie. A few tips:

- Winter squash can be stored on paper-lined shelves.
- Onions, shallots, and garlic do best in mesh bags because they need air circulation so they don't mold.
- Potatoes, carrots, beets, turnips, and rutabagas can go in wooden or cardboard boxes. Some folks bury them in layers using wood shavings or coarse sand, but it's not necessary unless your basement or garage has moisture issues and they'd otherwise be too wet.

Make a DIY garbage can "root cellar": You can fashion a root cellar of sorts with nothing more than a metal garbage can, wood shavings, and some sweat equity. Locate an area that has a bit of a slope if possible, so rain flows away from the top of the can when it's buried. Dig a hole a bit wider than the garbage can and only slightly shorter than the garbage can with the lid on. Set the garbage can into the hole and backfill with the soil around the sides of the can, sloping the dirt up at the sides to just the lip at the top of the garbage can. Fill the can with your vegetables, beginning with a layer of wood shavings and then a layer of vegetables. Continue layering in this way until you run out of veggies or reach the top of the can, ending with a layer of wood shavings. Place the lid back on the can, making sure the lid is on tight. Place some straw or hay over the lid in a thick layer. Over that, place a piece of plywood or hard insulation; hold it in place with a weight of some kind (two or three large rocks will do the trick).

Where to Store It All

A well-stocked pantry that can supply a family's needs for winter will take some serious space. Add in the space needed to store potable water, and you could easily double the area you'll need. You may be lucky enough to have a large garage, basement, laundry room, underused bedroom (such as a guest or craft room), or outside insulated shed, but many of us are not so fortunate. Even so, there are ways to get around a perceived lack of space. But wherever you stash your food and other essentials, just make sure that they are well contained, with tight-fitting lids, because you don't want to inadvertently "share" your food with unwanted bugs and critters. Especially if you live in a humid climate or—like me—live where the winters are wet—it's a good idea to place a desiccant packet in each container. I get mine online, and the cost is minimal.

Squirrel away canned goods, bags of flour, boxed mixes, and so forth in plastic tubs with fitted lids under your beds. If there is limited space under a bed, long and shallow gift wrap tubs usually fit; lay your cans, boxes, and bags in the tub, on their sides if needed to still allow you to close the lid. Closets are another great area to store things: Gallon jugs of water can easily be stored along the side and back walls without getting in the way. An empty drawer or cabinet shelf can house even more food, and you can hide a few items in seldom-used equipment (think large pots and canners). A storage bench by the front or back door or an ottoman with a top that opens make good spots too. If your hallway is wide enough, you can place sturdy, decorative cubbies or baskets along one edge. A little bit here, a little bit there, and suddenly you have quite a stash built up. And don't forget your walls! Adding some sturdy shelves can hold even more food.

Don't wait for an emergency to use your stash of food and water. Use it! As you use up your food, buy replacements so you never run out, and when you do replace something, remember to rotate your stores—first in equals first out. That way you'll never have to worry about freshness.

Note: I've arbitrarily used three months to mean "winter," and four people to equal "a family."

Methods for Safe Long-Term Storage

When the power goes out, suddenly our refrigerated and frozen food is at risk. But there are ways to nip this problem before it becomes a disaster, and that's with alternative storage methods:

Canning

Canning is one of the safest and surest methods for storing food long term. It's especially convenient for meat and poultry because those items are generally stored in your freezer. When the power goes out, you have about twenty-four hours for a half-filled freezer, or up to about forty-eight hours if your freezer is full, to either cook the meat or make other arrangements. You can lengthen that amount of time if you can get to a store for dry ice or block ice, but even then, you need to prioritize your freezer stash.

A dedicated pressure canner is the answer. But don't think you can make do with a large pot, because pressure canning requires temperatures higher than the boiling point to render low-acid food (such as meat, poultry, and many vegetables) safe to eat, and you need a pressure canner for that.

A perfect resource for all things canning, including more than 150 recipes, is another book of mine in this Homesteading series—*The Homestead Canning Cookbook* published by Harvest House Publishers. It's available from their website, harvesthousepublishers.com, or other online book retailers.

There are two canners I own and recommend, although there are others out on the market:

- ***Presto Pressure Canner and Cooker, 23-quart size***—Presto canners are relatively inexpensive compared to other brands and they are aluminum, which means they aren't as heavy as some other brands and therefore easier to move when filled with jars and water. If this size seems too heavy, Presto does make a 16-quart canner, but your canning output will be restricted because of the small size. The smaller Presto is actually on my wish list because I sometimes don't have a large amount of veggies or meat to can at a given time, and the 16-quart canner will come in handy for those smaller batches. I recommend that you have extra parts available at all times, such as a sealing ring gasket, overpressure plug, and steam gauge. The sealing ring gasket should be replaced once a year.

- *All American Pressure Canner/Cooker, 21.5-quart size*— All American canners are made to last a lifetime with proper care and maintenance. All American canners have a metal-to-metal sealing system instead of the usual gasket system. This was the first pressure canner I bought—more than forty years ago—and it's still in use. These canners are three times more expensive than Prestos, but they are extremely popular for a reason, so don't reject them out of hand due to price. They are quite a bit heavier than the Presto canners, so that might be a consideration for some. But they are absolute workhorses in the canning kitchen.

Dehydrating

Dehydrating is my favorite go-to for fruits of all kinds, especially apples, pears, bananas, strawberries, and prune plums. I take care to cut the fruit in thin slices as evenly as I can manage so they all dry at about the same rate. When the fruit is sufficiently dehydrated, I store them in canning jars with tight-fitting lids and add a desiccant packet to each jar. Vegetables that I like to dehydrate include carrots, onions, celery, potatoes, and tomatoes. I also dehydrate herbs and jerky.

While dehydrating is a form of long-term storage that I use regularly, I want to make clear that it's not foolproof. To successfully dehydrate food, you need to remove enough water so that yeast, mold, and harmful bacteria can't grow, and that's difficult to impossible for us to correctly determine at home. So, in our house, I use desiccant packets, keep the amounts in several different containers (in case one of them goes bad, I hopefully won't lose my entire stash), and freeze them until ready to use.

Some excellent dehydrator brands include Excalibur, Cosori, Nesco, Presto, Magic Mill, and Chefman. Most of these have additional trays you can buy for larger batches, and fruit leather tray inserts, which are handy for making fruit leather, which kids love.

You can also go low-tech with a solar dehydrator—purchase them online or find DIY plans if you want to build one yourself.

Freezing

Freezing food is a perfectly acceptable way to keep your larder stocked during winter—or anytime of the year. But when the power goes out, you have about forty-eight hours before the food will begin to go bad, and that's only if your freezer is full. With everything else that needs attention during an emergency, that's not long. Even so, freezing food works well, barring outages or if your freezer stops working.

The trick to freezing food is to remove as much air as you can before sealing the container, because air on the surface of your food causes dehydration and oxidation and contributes to freezer burn. Food won't be unsafe if there's freezer burn, but it will make meat and poultry tough and leathery. You can easily cut away the burned areas and eat the rest.

If you're interested in pursuing dehydration as a method of preserving food, you'll find this website especially informative, and the information is solid:

"Using Dehydration to Preserve Fruits, Vegetables, and Meats," VCE Publications, Virginia Tech, Virginia State University (vt.edu). https://www.pubs.ext.vt.edu/348/348-597/348-597.html.

The key is to wrap your food tightly, taking care to expel as much air as possible. Double wrapping is also very helpful. A vacuum sealer is ideal for keeping your frozen food fresh. But if you don't have one, double wrap with freezer paper, aluminum foil, or ziplock freezer bags. As you wrap the food, press the meat as you go so as little air as possible is inside.

Freeze-Drying

Freeze-drying is yet another option for long-term storage of many foods. If you're interested in using this process for your food storage plans, you can find lots of information online. The variety of foods that can be freeze-dried is staggering (ice cream sandwiches, anyone?), and whereas dehydrating can extract as little as 70 percent of the water in food, freeze-drying extracts about 98 percent—a vast improvement that radically extends shelf life. Freeze-drying retains more nutrients, and when the food is rehydrated, it more closely approximates the taste and texture of fresh.

At one point, I was highly interested in this method of food preservation, but in the end, I decided against it. My reasons included cost of the machine, cost of use, the size of the appliance, and the noise while using. (It's as loud as a vacuum cleaner, and the run time can average twenty to forty hours per batch.) It just doesn't fit with my approach to life. However, I know someone who has a home freeze dryer, uses it often, and loves it.

Aseptic Packaging

Aseptic packaging is a food processing technique that allows certain liquid products to be shelf-stable (no refrigeration needed if unopened) for six months to a year. Common aseptically packaged liquids include milk, broth, tofu, plant-based beverages such as soy, almond, and oat milk, liquid eggs, whipping cream, soup, and tomatoes. I regularly keep broth, soy milk, and tofu in my pantry and love the convenience. Aseptic packaged foods can be bought at any grocery store.

THE PANTRY ESSENTIALS LIST

Now let's get down to specifics. This next section lists what I consider to be winter pantry essentials and the estimated amounts of each item needed for a winter *for a family of four* without going to a store or restaurant. Remember that this list isn't exhaustive, and depending on personal tastes, your winter pantry might end up different than mine. Hopefully, however, this will get you off to a great start.

Again, pull out your notebook and write down what you still need. I've added a box beside each item below—use the boxes to check off the items you already have or that you will purchase in the future.

Flour and Grains

To successfully store flour and grains, you'll need food-grade buckets with tight-fitting lids to keep out insects. For smaller amounts, quart, half-gallon, and gallon canning jars work well also. (You can use the metal lids that come with the jars, or better yet, buy plastic screw-on tops made especially for canning jars, as metal lids do tend to rust over time.) Make sure there are no tears in the packaging (wrap them thoroughly with plastic if there are). Immediately put flour and grains into your freezer for two to three days to kill any bugs present (see *Note on next page*). Next, pour the flour or grains into the buckets or jars and secure the lids. I always add desiccant packets to the *bottom* of my containers before pouring in the flour or grains. There are different-sized desiccant packets to match your container sizes, but I simply buy a large package of one size and use two to three desiccant packets for my three- and five-gallon buckets.

❏ *Unbleached White Flour:* I recommend storing white flour because whole wheat flour can go rancid quickly. Plan on storing about 60 to 100 pounds of flour. That may seem like a lot, but homemade bread can easily use a pound of flour per loaf, and you'll want extra to make baked goods like cookies and cakes, bulk mixes, or to thicken sauces and gravy.

❏ *Whole Wheat Flour:* Whole wheat flour can go rancid in about three to six months if stored in your pantry. But if you have your heart set on using whole wheat flour, a ten-pound bag will easily last for a winter. If you exclusively use whole wheat flour instead of white flour, figure on about 100 pounds to get you through. Personally, I don't buy whole wheat flour—instead, I prefer to grind my own wheat berries as I need them to get around the concern about rancidity.

❏ *Wheat Berries:* If you decide to store wheat berries, you'll need a grain mill to turn the wheat berries into whole wheat flour. This is what I choose to do. An electric grain mill makes grinding flour quick and easy, but during an emergency, there might not be electricity, so

Note: You might have heard that you can eliminate a weevil or mite infestation in your flour by sifting the bugs out using a fine-mesh sifter. I don't recommend it, however, because even though the bugs can be sifted out, the eggs they leave behind can't. Still, you *can* use the sifted flour in baking because the high temperatures will kill any lingering eggs. So take the time to freeze your flour and grains, and check your buckets every so often to make sure they're still good.

a hand-cranked grain mill is a must. Hand-cranked mills take muscle and time to produce enough flour for baking, and I can't stress enough that buying the best you can afford will make the difference between using the grain mill or letting it sit around gathering dust. I have both an electric mill and a hand-cranked mill, and I use both, even when the power isn't out. Here are some grain mills I have owned and loved:

- Recommended electric grain mills: WonderMill, NutriMill
- Recommended hand-cranked grain mills: Country Living, Diamant

❏ *Hard white winter wheat* is my favorite go-to. It makes fabulous bread but can also be used for baking just about anything that uses flour. I use it to make bread, tortillas, sweet bread, cookies, and noodles. Often, I use a combination of wheat flour and unbleached white flour because the younger members of my family prefer the lighter taste and texture.

❏ *Soft white spring wheat* is lower in protein and has a lighter texture and flavor. It works best for pancakes, muffins, biscuits, cakes, cookies, and pastries.

❏ *Durum wheat* is the hardest wheat of all and is used primarily for pasta. But unless you're itching to try this variety and make your own pasta from scratch, I don't think it's necessary to add durum to your grains stash (even though I do!). Instead, use your hard white wheat.

Store about sixty pounds of wheat berries. But let's face it—not everybody wants the expense of a grain mill so they can grind their own grain. If you decide this isn't for you, add another fifty pounds of unbleached white flour to your total and call it good.

❏ *Pasta:* We easily go through thirty-five-plus pounds of noodles each winter, but it's fair to say that we eat more pasta than most. But for a family of four, you'll use a half pound of dry pasta per meal, so ten pounds (which will provide twenty pasta meals over the course of the winter) is probably enough, especially if you also stock a few pounds of assorted noodles, such as egg noodles and elbow macaroni.

❏ *Oatmeal:* Oatmeal can last a very long time in storage, so I always have about fifty pounds on hand. But for a winter pantry, twenty-five pounds should be plenty, unless you eat oatmeal for breakfast every morning. If so, double that amount. I used to be an oatmeal snob and rolled my own oat groats fresh each time. I do love fresh rolled oats, but it turns out the oil in the groats can turn rancid quickly. So now I store already-rolled oatmeal. Live and learn.

❏ *Rice:* Again, I keep white versus brown rice because white rice won't go rancid. And I'll be honest—we all love white rice way more than brown. There are two cups of uncooked rice per pound, and that pound will yield about six cups cooked, which will handily feed our hypothetical family of four. So, figure on about a pound of rice per meal. Storing twenty-five pounds will net a family of four at least twenty-five meals, and that should be plenty.

❏ *Cornmeal:* Plan on twenty pounds. Corn bread, anyone? (I have a great bulk corn bread mix recipe on page 72.)

❏ *Masa Harina:* Masa harina is simply cornmeal that has been processed in a different way from regular cornmeal. The process (called nixtamalization) produces the unique taste and texture of corn tortillas and tamales. You can pick up a four-and-a-half-pound bag (or thereabouts) at any grocery store, and that should be enough.

❏ *Miscellaneous Flours and Grains:* There are many varieties of flour and grains, and if you love something, add it to your stash. For instance, we like pearled barley, quinoa, couscous, and buckwheat flour, so they go into our pantry as well, usually about a half gallon at a time.

Eggs and Dairy

❏ *Eggs:* Even if you have chickens, they go through a molt, usually in the fall, when they lose old feathers and grow new ones in preparation for better insulation during the cold months of winter. During the molt, chickens drastically reduce their egg production and often stop laying completely. This can take weeks or even a couple months. So there will be times when you don't have access to eggs. Of course, you could go to the store and buy a dozen, but what if you can't?

Help can be had in the form of #10 cans of *dehydrated scrambled eggs* for rehydrating, cooking, and eating, and *pasteurized whole egg powder* used for cooking. (In fact, baking cakes, brownies, etc. using whole egg powder seems to make my baked goods lighter and fluffier. Win!) I buy a 14-ounce bag online, which gives me the equivalent of thirty-two eggs that I only use for baking and lasts me for several months. It's rather expensive, but I truly believe the benefits are worth the expense.

❏ *Milk:* So many uses!

❏ *Instant nonfat dry milk* is incredibly useful to have on hand. You can use it for drinking, cooking, and making bulk mixes (see the chapter called Bulk Mixes). One #10 can is a bare minimum, but two cans ensures that you won't run out anytime soon, and if you intend to drink it, get a third can.

❏ *Powdered buttermilk* is very useful as well. You can buy 12-ounce tubs of cultured dry buttermilk powder at grocery stores or online. I keep two tubs on hand, and once I open a container, I throw in a desiccant pack because for some reason, my powdered buttermilk tends to clump.

❏ *Aseptically packaged (shelf stable) milk* is another useful pantry essential, and cartons are good for about six months if unopened. I haven't yet bought aseptically packaged heavy cream, but I'm thinking I need to try it because adding cream to my morning coffee will make any day better!

❏ *Butter:* Refrigerated butter can last a long time, and you can freeze it so it lasts longer still. But when refrigeration isn't available, butter powder is your go-to—definitely another must-have in your winter pantry. You can use it to make sauces and gravies, add to baked goods, sprinkle over vegetables, and toss with salt when making popcorn. Two pounds will last the winter. I usually buy mine online, but you can also pick up a container at many grocery stores.

❏ *Cheese:* Unfortunately, even hard cheeses need to be refrigerated, with just a few exceptions and in certain circumstances. But as with most things, there are ways to circumvent this problem when refrigeration isn't available:

> ❏ *Processed cheese* can be stored unrefrigerated for months. American cheese and various cheese spreads are useful to have around if you don't mind some of the ingredients. They tend to melt easily.

> ❏ *Cheese powder* is so convenient to keep on hand. You can sprinkle it on popcorn, vegetables, and eggs, and use it to make a tasty cheese sauce for all sorts of recipes.

Beans and Other Legumes

I love beans! They are inexpensive, high in protein and fiber, low in calories, cholesterol-free, and full of vitamins and minerals. Eat a meal that features beans, and you'll feel full thanks to the fiber.

You can mix and match the types of beans you store. Favorites include pinto beans, black beans, red and pink kidney beans, small white beans (also called great northern or navy beans), lentils, split peas, baby limas, and garbanzo beans (also called chickpeas).

Next, decide in what form you will store them. Dry beans take up less room but need water and a long cook time to process. They are also cheaper to purchase in dry form. Canned beans are already cooked, but they'll need more storage room. I buy bulk amounts of dry beans and home can them so they are ready to go when needed.

❑ Store about three gallons of dried beans or thirty (14.5 ounce) cans of whatever beans you like best.

❑ Lentils should be added to your pantry because they're tasty and cook up fairly quickly. Store a quart or two.

Meat and Fish

Meat is tricky because it needs to be eaten fresh or frozen for later use. But what happens if the power goes out for an extended period? The potential for loss is great. I solve this dilemma by freezing some and canning some. Half of one of our freezers is filled with meat, and while I've never lost frozen meat in an unexpected thaw, I'm always prepared for that eventuality. I have cases of empty, clean canning jars and a propane camp stove that I use for canning. I figure if the worst happens, I'll pressure can the meat when it's thawed. Yes, we'll have to move quickly, and my family will be conscripted into being temporary kitchen helpers, but we'll be able to save most if not all of it.

Plan on roughly a half pound of meat per person per day. At this rate, our average family of four would need two pounds of meat available per day, or 180 pounds of meat to last the winter. We will round up this figure to 200 pounds for our hypothetical family for the winter. Another interesting fact that we will take into consideration is that North Americans eat the following types of meat in descending order from most to least: chicken, followed by beef, and then pork. There are obviously other types of meat as well as fish and seafood, but these are the mainstays in the American diet, so we will fill our freezer with these three, plus canned tuna. Just remember that you can store much or even all your meat requirement as canned meat instead of frozen.

❑ *Chicken:* Eighty pounds of chicken pieces and whole chickens in any configuration your family prefers.

❑ *Ground Beef:* Sixty pounds of ground beef/hamburger

❑ *Beef Roasts and Steaks:* Twenty-five pounds of beef roasts and steaks

❑ *Pork:* Fifteen pounds of pork, stored as roast, chops, or sausage

❑ *Canned Tuna (or Canned Salmon if you prefer):* We can our own fresh tuna and get as many as forty jars per season, which we always use. But for those of you who want an easier way, buy two eight-packs of canned tuna each fall. Our family uses tuna to make sandwiches, creamed tuna on toast, and tuna noodle casserole. You can also add it to salads and make tuna chowder—there are many ways to use this tasty fish!

❑ *Salt-Cured Meat:* Salt-cured meat like salami, pepperoni, jerky, and summer sausage can sit on your pantry shelf for months if unopened. And while it can be unrefrigerated, it's still best to store it in a cool, dark place. Several pounds would be a great addition to your food stores.

Sweeteners

❑ *Granulated Sugar:* Buy one or two ten-pound bags and store the sugar with a desiccant packet in a three- to five-gallon bucket with a tight-fitting lid or use several gallon jars.

❑ *Brown Sugar:* Store two to four pounds; place in airtight containers. To keep the brown sugar from drying out and getting hard, wet a decorative brown sugar saver or a very clean clay pot shard before placing it on top of the brown sugar and close tight. Each time you open the container to use some sugar, rewet the shard/sugar saver before replacing it in the container.

❑ *Honey:* We sometimes use honey on pancakes, waffles, toast, and bagels, and for sweetening tea, so three 16-ounce bottles works for us. If you bake with honey, you'll likely need more than that.

❑ *Maple Syrup:* Maple syrup can be used for more than just

pancakes and waffles. It flavors baked goods, oatmeal, yogurt, bacon, salad dressing, and whatever else you can think of. Pick up a couple of quarts at the beginning of winter, and you're good to go.

❑ *Powdered Sugar:* A two-pound bag should be enough and will fill a half-gallon jar.

Oil and Shortening

❑ *Vegetable Shortening:* We use Crisco brand shortening in our house, but lard is nice to have on hand for things like pie crusts and biscuits. Plan on storing two three-pound cans or add a third can if you plan on making a lot of bulk mixes.

❑ *Cooking Oil:* Store one gallon of vegetable and/or olive oil. We like avocado oil because it has a higher smoke point, so we tend to store a half gallon each of vegetable and avocado oil, and then add a couple of bottles of olive oil.

Vegetables

❑ *Fresh Vegetables:* If our only "shopping" opportunities came from our pantries for an entire winter, we'd soon hanker for something fresh. Thankfully, there are vegetables that are considered long keepers and will last for most of the winter when kept in a cool, dark place out of direct light:

potatoes	sweet potatoes	carrots	onions
garlic	beets	turnips	hot peppers
celery root	rutabagas	thick-skinned winter squash such as acorn, delicata, pumpkin, Hubbard, or butternut	
See the material in the Gardening section on page 28 for more information.			

❏ *Canned Vegetables:* Canned vegetables can be eaten plain or added to soups, stews, and casseroles. Plan on storing at least one can per day, so for three months, that would equal ninety cans.

❏ *Spaghetti Sauce:* When tomatoes are ripe in summer, I spend countless hours processing tomatoes and canning tomato sauce. My goal is to put up at least 100 jars (quarts and pints) of sauce to see us through until next year. For a winter pantry, however, you only need about thirty to forty home-canned quart jars, or two twelve-packs of store-bought sauce (about fifteen ounces per can).

❏ *Dehydrated and Freeze-Dried Vegetables:* I always keep dehydrated mixed vegetables on hand. I mostly use them in winter soups and stews, because I don't always have access to fresh vegetables. I order organic dehydrated veggies online, and usually have at least a quart stored away in my pantry.

❏ *Sprouts:* In the deep, dark winter, I sometimes just yearn for the taste of summer. Sprouts are my answer. Going into winter, I make sure to have a pound of organic sprouting seeds on hand—usually a mix of alfalfa, clover, broccoli, and radish—and I will often simply grab a small handful of finished sprouts and eat them plain. But sprouts can be layered into a sandwich, thrown into a pot of soup at the last minute, or dipped in salad dressing (ranch and balsamic vinaigrette are my favorites) and eaten along with a meal.

Another plus is that sprouts are quick and easy to grow. Here is my basic method:

Rinse about one and a half tablespoons of sprouts and place them in the bottom of a very clean quart canning jar. Fill the jar with cool water and put a sprouting lid or several thicknesses of a nylon stocking or small-mesh cheesecloth on the top. Set it on your counter and let the seeds soak for several hours. Pour out the water, gently shake the jar to remove as much water as possible, and then spread the sprouts around the side of the jar as best you can. Carefully tilt the jar, lid side down, into a bowl just far enough that the water can continue to drain completely but the seeds don't fall in a heap at the bottom. Set the jar in a dark area (I usually put it in a cupboard, but a dark corner of your kitchen will do).

Three times a day (four times a day if the weather is hot), without removing the sprouting lid, fill the jar with cool water, gently swish the sprouts, drain the water, shake to spread the sprouts onto the side of the jar, and then once again tilt the jar into the bowl to continue draining. On day three or four, move the sprouting jar into indirect sunlight to let the sprouts green up; continue to rinse and drain as you have been doing. Your sprouts should be ready in five to six days. When complete, take your sprouts and swish them by hand in a large bowl with fresh water; this will give them a final rinse and help to remove the seed hulls. Lay the sprouts on a paper towel or dish towel and spread them out to dry for a bit. Store your finished sprouts in a container with a folded paper towel at the bottom to continue to wick out moisture, place in the refrigerator, and eat within about five days.

Fruit

Fresh fruit is mainly a summer food, but you can buy apples, pears, citrus, and green bananas during the winter months and they will last for a month or two if kept in a cool, dark place out of direct sunlight. But when you can't get to the store, an emergency stash of canned fruit is just the ticket. Eat the canned fruit plain, in yogurt, or as an ingredient in fruit cobblers and other baked goods. (See the recipe section for recipe ideas.)

❏ *Canned fruit:* Buy a total of twenty-five cans of various canned fruits such as peaches, pears, fruit cocktail, or pineapple.

❏ *Raisins:* A two-pound box of raisins will suffice for snacking and adding to oatmeal, granola, and baked goods.

Salt and Pepper

❏ *Salt:* Table salt comes in either plain or iodized form. Take your pick but get two pounds. I buy iodized salt for the table and cooking, but I also keep a stash of plain salt for my canning and pickling needs. Many folks prefer using sea salt and if you're one of them, get sea salt. I don't use it, because in my climate sea salt tends to clump, but cook's choice.

❏ *Black Pepper:* Pepper isn't as necessary as salt, but it's a useful spice to keep on hand. Eight ounces should be more than enough for normal use.

Herbs, Spices, Seasonings, and Miscellaneous Pantry Items

The herbs, spices, seasonings, and miscellany in the list on the right are essential for baking, cooking, and making your meals tasty, so get as many as you can. Don't forget to add what your family uses regularly if it's not on this list. Examples of some of our personal favorites are Creole seasoning, za'atar, tarragon, coriander, and caraway.

Estimate how much you'll use during an entire winter and plan accordingly. Make a note of the "best by" date and mark it on the container. Remember that spices will stay fresh longer when stored in a dark place away from heat (so a cabinet next to your stove isn't ideal).

Make a checkmark next to each of the spices and kitchen items on the checklist on the right once you have purchased the item.

- ❏ Active dry yeast
- ❏ Aluminum foil
- ❏ Apple cider vinegar
- ❏ Baking powder
- ❏ Balsamic vinegar
- ❏ Basil
- ❏ Bay leaves
- ❏ Beef bouillon
- ❏ Black pepper
- ❏ Can opener, non-electric
- ❏ Cardamom
- ❏ Chicken bouillon
- ❏ Chili powder
- ❏ Cinnamon
- ❏ Cloves
- ❏ Coffee
- ❏ Corn starch
- ❏ Cream of tartar
- ❏ Creamer
- ❏ Crushed red pepper
- ❏ Cumin
- ❏ Curry powder
- ❏ Garlic, minced and/ or powder
- ❏ Ginger
- ❏ Italian seasoning
- ❏ Lighter and fluid
- ❏ Matches
- ❏ Mustard, ground
- ❏ Mustard, yellow
- ❏ Nutmeg
- ❏ Onion powder
- ❏ Oregano
- ❏ Paprika, smoked and sweet
- ❏ Parsley
- ❏ Peanut butter
- ❏ Plastic wrap
- ❏ Poppy seeds
- ❏ Potatoes, fresh and dehydrated mashed
- ❏ Rosemary
- ❏ Sage
- ❏ Salt
- ❏ Sesame seeds
- ❏ Summer savory
- ❏ Taco seasoning
- ❏ Tea
- ❏ Thyme
- ❏ Turmeric
- ❏ Unsweetened cocoa powder
- ❏ Vanilla extract
- ❏ Vegetable bouillon
- ❏ White vinegar
- ❏ Ziplock bags

HEALTH
AND MEDICINE

When winter sets in, and if anyone in your family relies on **prescription medicines or equipment**, getting your prescriptions filled could become problematic during an emergency. Talk with your health care practitioner about possible solutions. Keep in mind that the answers will likely vary depending on your particular circumstances—the state or territory you live in, your insurance provider, and the type of medication you're seeking, especially if it's a controlled substance. Once you have some answers, you'll be better able to make informed decisions about what to do should disaster strike and hopefully have enough to see you through an emergency.

If at least one family member is properly trained in **CPR**, their knowledge and skills will greatly improve the chances for a positive outcome in a medical emergency. When a situation is handled with calm expedience, the responder's confidence to stay unruffled and help the victim will likely transfer to onlookers.

Without any special training, there's much you can do to prepare for the everyday illnesses, aches and pains, and small injuries that are bound to happen. That's when a first aid kit comes in handy, and every household should have one.

First Aid Kit

You can certainly buy a first aid kit—some of them are amazingly complete, and they come in a handy tote. But making your own isn't that hard, and it'll likely be less expensive. Here's a list of some basic supplies to keep on hand:

❏ Activated charcoal

❏ Antibacterial hand wipes

❏ Antibiotic ointment

❏ Antibiotic towelettes

❏ Baking soda

❏ Bandages, various sizes

❏ Bandaging tape

❏ Calamine lotion

❏ Eye wash

❏ Gauze dressings

❏ Hydrocortisone cream

❏ Hydrogen peroxide

❏ Over-the-counter pain relievers

❏ Rubbing alcohol

❏ Scissors

❏ Soap

❏ Sterile gloves

❏ Sunscreen

❏ Thermometer

❏ Tweezers

❏ Wash cloths

❏ Witch hazel

Cold and Flu Medicine

Having over-the-counter cold and flu medicine can help control symptoms and make patients more comfortable as they're healing. Here's a list of common types to add to your medicine cabinet.

❏ Antacid

❏ Antidiarrheal medicine

❏ Antihistamine

❏ Cough drops

❏ Cough medicine/ suppressant

❏ Decongestant

❏ Kleenex

❏ Nighttime cold and flu

❏ Vitamin C

❏ Zinc

Not Feeling Well? There's a Recipe for That!

Homemade remedies can have a place in your winter homestead. You might be stuck at home due to inclement weather, or, like me, you prefer to care for minor ailments and injuries yourself, instead of rushing to the doctor at the first sign of illness.

Now I'll be quick to admit that modern medical technology has many advantages in certain situations, and I hope you think the same. But when common colds, flu, aches and pains, or anxious times occur, your first line of defense might just be found in your kitchen cupboard. Often, there are natural and inexpensive relief options for what ails you.

Here are some of the homegrown remedies we use in our family.

ONION AND HONEY COUGH SYRUP

Onions have expectorant, antibiotic, and anti-inflammatory properties, all of which work well to subdue your cough, while honey coats and soothes your throat.

1 to 2 onions

Honey

Slice the onion very thinly and place the slices evenly in a saucepan. Don't use aluminum, which is reactive. Pour in just enough honey to barely cover the onion slices. Cover the saucepan and heat the mixture for about 45 minutes to an hour on the lowest heat setting possible so the bottom of the saucepan doesn't scorch. (You might need to remove the saucepan from the heat for a few minutes here and there to keep the mixture from scorching.)

Don't strain out the onions. Instead place the mixture in a covered jar and refrigerate. (It will last all winter.)

To use: Take a spoonful at a time as often as you need to.

DECONGESTANT

2 tsp. dried peppermint leaves or 2 T. chopped fresh

1 tsp. dried rosemary, heaping

1 tsp. dried thyme, heaping

1 quart water

In a saucepan, add the peppermint, rosemary, and thyme to the water. Bring to a boil and then turn off the heat and cover the pot, letting the mixture steep for several minutes.

Remove the cover from the pot and then drape a towel over your head. Before you get close to the pot, ensure that the steam isn't too hot, and don't get so close that the steam burns you. Then lean over the pot so the towel tents in such a way that the steam gets caught inside the towel. Close your eyes and breathe in the aroma. Breathe in the steam for several minutes and repeat as necessary. (You don't need to make a fresh batch—simply reheat the mixture and use again, covering the pot between sessions.) The steam helps to moisturize and soothe your nostrils while the herbs act as natural decongestants.

ECHINACEA IMMUNE BOOSTER TEA

1¼ cups water

1 T. dried echinacea or 2 T. fresh

Honey to taste (optional)

Lemon juice to taste (optional)

Echinacea, also called purple coneflower, is a beautiful flowering plant. You can grow your own and dry the flowers to make tea, but it's easy to buy the dried flowers at an herb store or online. Stock up in the fall so you don't run out. Echinacea tea is good anytime, but if you think you've been in contact with someone who is now sick, drink a cup or two a day for several days to strengthen your immune system and hopefully stave off getting a cold yourself.

In a small saucepan, bring the water to a boil. Add the echinacea, cover the pot, remove from the heat, and let steep for 5 to 10 minutes. Pour into a mug and add optional honey and lemon to taste.

ELDERBERRY COLD AND FLU TEA

When I start feeling ill, I immediately start dosing myself with elderberry tea, and it often reduces the severity of symptoms and duration of my illness. I drink two cups a day until my symptoms disappear.

2 cups water

2 T. dried elderberries

1 small piece of cinnamon stick (about 1 inch long)

In a small saucepan, heat the water and elderberries just to boiling. Immediately turn down the heat and gently simmer for about 10 minutes. Turn off the heat, add the cinnamon stick, cover the saucepan, and let it rest for 5 minutes. Strain the tea through a fine-mesh strainer and drink.

SORE THROAT GARGLE

If a sore throat is plaguing you, here are several different combinations that will work wonders for easing the pain and rawness.

- Place about ½ teaspoon of table salt into a drinking glass or cup. Add hot water and stir until the salt has mostly dissolved. Gargle with the salt water (the warmer, the better) and spit out. Repeat this several times and then rinse your mouth if the saltiness bothers you. (You can also add ¼ teaspoon of turmeric spice to this gargle for added benefit.)
- Mix 1 teaspoon of lemon juice in ½ cup of hot water. Gargle several times.
- Add 5 shakes of hot sauce or cayenne pepper to a cup of hot water, stir, and then gargle. Depending on how raw your throat is, this could sting, but the capsaicin in the pepper will soon bring relief.
- Add 1 teaspoon of apple cider vinegar to ½ cup of hot water. Gargle several times and then drink the last little bit.

WHITE WILLOW BARK TEA FEVER REDUCER AND ANTI-INFLAMMATORY

1 to 2 tsp. white willow bark

1 cup water

Honey to taste

Note: White willow bark has salicin, which is very similar to aspirin (salicylic acid) and works the same way. If you are taking medication that requires you to not ingest aspirin or if you have surgery scheduled in the near future, you'll want to stay away from this tea.

(You can double or triple this recipe if you want to make several cups at once.)

Place the bark and water in a saucepan and bring to a boil. Cover the pot, turn the heat down, and simmer for 10 minutes; turn off the heat, keeping the pot covered, and allow the bark to continue steeping for 30 minutes.

Strain the tea and add honey to taste. Drink up to four cups daily. It will take some time before you find relief, so be patient. On the plus side, the positive effects of drinking the tea will last a good long while.

6

COMMUNICATION, TRAVEL, AND ENTERTAINMENT

Communication

Power outages can affect our ability to communicate with those not immediately around us. So what are ways we can communicate with others when the power goes out and the internet is down? And how can we get much-needed news updates?

If you have phone service, limit non-emergency phone calls—only call if necessary and keep your calls short, because it's very likely that there will be a high volume of calls putting stress on cellular services. Text messages can sometimes go through when a phone call can't, so try a variety of services for better success.

Here's my list of alternate ways to communicate in an emergency:

❏ Battery-powered or hand-cranked radio that has the NOAA weather band included

❏ Landline telephone

❏ Social media

❏ Two-way radios

❏ Citizens band (CB) radio

❏ HAM radio

❏ Police scanner

Before the need arises, make a list (not digital) of all emergency phone numbers. Keep it in an easily accessed spot and let everyone know where it is.

Travel

Travel during an emergency might very well be impossible, but if you need to evacuate or otherwise leave from where you are, the single most important thing to consider is having enough gas for the trip. A good rule of thumb is to always keep at least half a tank of gas in your vehicles. Don't be the person who slides into the gas station running on fumes before filling up.

If you store the following items in your vehicles, you'll be in good shape if you get stranded somewhere:

❏ Blankets

❏ Car cell phone charger

❏ Small first aid kit (you can make your own)

❏ Flashlight with extra batteries

❏ Jumper cable

❏ Bottled water

❏ Snacks

❏ Flares or reflective road triangle

❏ Sand or cat litter for traction

❏ Weather-related items (ice scraper, umbrella, rainproof poncho, etc.)

Entertainment

Many of us spend a great deal of time on our various devices, but what to do when the internet goes down and the power is out? Here are some suggestions:

- ❏ Draw or paint
- ❏ Play "I Spy" guessing game
- ❏ Play bingo
- ❏ Play board games
- ❏ Play cards
- ❏ Play charades
- ❏ Read aloud to the whole family
- ❏ Read silently
- ❏ Play "Simon Says"
- ❏ Rock, paper, scissors
- ❏ Take a walk
- ❏ Tell stories

PART THREE

RECIPES

When I think of winter and cooking, I think comfort food—hearty, filling, and warming. Coming inside after a cold day to a warm meal is the epitome of coziness and well-being. The following recipes fit the bill, and many of the ingredients star winter-centric items. Many of the recipes also take advantage of your winter pantry preps—no need to run to the store, because you'll have everything you need to create fantastic meals.

Most of the recipes in this section are quick and easy—what I call my old standbys. With these recipes, there's no need to spend hours in the kitchen—and you'll turn out tasty meals for your family in no time.

BULK MIXES

There are many reasons to make your own homemade bulk mixes. They cost less than their store-bought counterparts, they taste good, they save you time, and you know exactly what's in them. And if you run out of one of these mixes, chances are good that you can replenish the supply without a trip to the grocery store. It's a good feeling!

I've been making and using homemade mixes for more than forty years, and I still get a thrill when my shelves are filled. Need a housewarming, birthday, or holiday gift for a friend? Fill a gallon jar with a favorite mix, attach a recipe card with a pretty ribbon, and your gift is ready to go.

Storing your mixes is easy. I use half-gallon and gallon jars, but you can just as easily use gallon freezer or storage bags. (They take up less shelf space, but I prefer jars because I can use them again and again.) These mixes will stay fresh longer when stored in a cool, dry place.

One last plus? You've already done most of the measuring and blending of ingredients, so meal prep is a breeze.

HOMEMADE BAKING POWDER (LARGE BATCH)

1 part cornstarch or arrowroot powder	*If you want to make a large amount to have on hand, follow this "recipe":*
1 part cream of tartar	Mix well and store in an airtight container or storage bag.
½ part baking soda	

2 tsp. cornstarch or arrowroot powder	*If you just need a small amount for a single recipe, follow this "recipe":*
2 tsp. cream of tartar	Mix well and store in an airtight container or storage bag or use immediately.
1 tsp. baking soda	

MASTER BISCUIT MIX

8½ cups flour	In a large mixing bowl, sift together all dry ingredients, mixing very well. With a pastry blender, cut the shortening into the dry ingredients until evenly distributed and the consistency resembles coarse cornmeal. Place in an airtight container or gallon-sized bag. Date the container; it's best to use the mix within three months, but I've kept it longer with no ill effects.
3 T. baking powder	
1 T. salt	
2 tsp. cream of tartar	
1 tsp. baking soda	
1½ cups instant nonfat dry milk	
2¼ cups shortening	

This Master Biscuit Mix can be used whenever a recipe calls for Bisquick™ or another all-purpose baking mix.

TRADITIONAL ROLLED BISCUITS

Preheat the oven to 450°.

In a large bowl, mix ingredients together. Cover the dough and let it rest for 5 minutes. Turn out onto a lightly floured surface and knead gently about 15 times. Roll out the dough to 1½-inch thickness and cut with a floured biscuit cutter. Place about 2 inches apart on an ungreased cookie sheet and bake for 10 to 12 minutes.

3 cups Master Biscuit Mix

⅔ cup milk or water

DROP BISCUITS

Preheat the oven to 450°.

Grease a cookie sheet and set aside. In a mixing bowl, mix ingredients together; stir just until blended. Drop dough by tablespoonfuls onto the greased cookie sheet and bake for 8 to 10 minutes.

3 cups Master Biscuit Mix

¾ cup milk or water

QUICK AND EASY PIZZA CRUST

Preheat the oven to 425°.

Mix dry ingredients; add water and turn out dough on a lightly floured surface. Let stand 5 minutes. Knead dough about 20 times and then pat dough into a greased pizza pan. Top with your favorite pizza sauce and toppings and bake for 20 minutes or until done.

3¼ cups Master Biscuit Mix

2¼ tsp. (1 packet) active dry yeast

½ tsp. salt

¼ tsp. garlic powder (optional)

¼ tsp. dried basil (optional)

¾ cup warm water (about 100° to 110°)

MASTER BROWNIE MIX

6 cups flour

4 tsp. baking powder

4 tsp. salt

8 cups sugar

1 (8-oz.) can unsweetened baking cocoa powder

2 cups shortening

In a large mixing bowl, sift together the flour, baking powder, and salt. Add the sugar and cocoa and mix well again. Add the shortening and work with a pastry cutter or two forks until the shortening has been well incorporated and the mixture resembles coarse cornmeal. Place in an airtight container or large plastic storage bag. Date the container and use within three to four months.

BROWNIES

Preheat the oven to 350°.

Grease and flour an 8 × 8-inch baking dish.

In a medium mixing bowl, combine the eggs, vanilla, and Master Brownie Mix. Beat by hand or with a mixer until smooth. Stir in nuts or chocolate chips if using. Pour batter into prepared pan and bake for 30 to 35 minutes. Cool before cutting. When ready to serve, sprinkle top with a dusting of powdered sugar.

2 eggs, beaten

1 tsp. vanilla

2½ cups Master Brownie Mix

½ cup chopped nuts (optional)

¼ to ½ cup chocolate chips (optional)

Powdered sugar for dusting

CHEWY CHOCOLATE COOKIES

Preheat the oven to 375°. Grease a cookie sheet and set aside for now.

In a medium mixing bowl, combine eggs and water. Beat well by hand, using a fork to help break up and disperse the eggs. Stir in the Master Brownie Mix, baking soda, flour, and vanilla and blend well again.

Drop by teaspoonfuls onto the prepared cookie sheet, about 2 inches apart. Lightly push a walnut or pecan half (if using) into the top of each cookie. Bake for 10 to 12 minutes.

Variations: Roll dough in powdered sugar before placing onto cookie sheet; press nuts into the top and bake as above.

2 eggs, beaten

½ cup water

2¼ cups Master Brownie Mix

½ tsp. baking soda

¾ cup flour

1 tsp. vanilla

Walnut or pecan halves (optional)

CAESAR DRESSING (LARGE BATCH)

2 cups mayonnaise

1 head garlic, cloves separated, peeled, and roughly chopped

1 (2 oz.) can anchovy fillets, roughly chopped

2 generous pinches of salt

⅓ cup lemon juice

1 T. Dijon mustard

1 T. Worcestershire sauce

3 oz. finely grated Parmigiano-Reggiano cheese (about 1 cup)

Generous amount of black pepper

3 T. water

My brother developed this recipe, and it's the best Caesar dressing, bar none, that I've ever tasted.

Using a stick blender, food processor, or other tool, combine all ingredients and blend until desired texture is achieved.

Refrigerate in an airtight container and use within about three weeks.

MASTER CAKE MIX

3⅓ cups shortening, room temperature

7⅔ cups sugar, divided

11 cups sifted flour

5 T. baking powder

3 T. salt

Place shortening in a large mixing bowl. With a mixer set at medium speed, cream the shortening for half a minute. Scrape the sides and bottom of the bowl and mix for another half minute at the same speed.

Add 4 cups of the sugar, 1 cup at a time, mixing after each addition, at medium speed for 1 minute.

In another very large mixing bowl, sift together the flour, baking powder, salt, and remaining 3⅔ cups of sugar. Add 2 cups of this sifted mixture into the bowl with the shortening and sugar mixture; beat at medium speed for half a minute.

Add the shortening mixture to the large bowl that contains the dry ingredients and mix until it looks like coarse cornmeal and is very well blended. (You can use your mixer, but you might need to finish by hand.)

To store the cake mix: You can store the entire master cake mix in a large airtight container or measure the mix into 6 equal portions of 3½ cups each by measuring carefully as you spoon the mix into a measuring cup; be sure to not pack the mix down. Use quart jars with lids or ziplock bags and store in a cool, dark place. The mixes should last several months, but you can freeze them for a longer shelf life.

YELLOW CAKE

3½ cups Master Cake Mix

2 medium eggs, beaten

¾ cup milk

1 tsp. vanilla

Preheat the oven to 350°. Grease two 8-inch cake pans or one 10 × 13-inch baking dish.

Place the mix into a two-quart bowl. Make a well in the center of the mix and add the eggs, milk, and vanilla. Beat for 1 minute with an electric mixer set at low speed. Scrape sides and bottom of the bowl and beat for 2 minutes more. Batter should be smooth and free of lumps.

Pour the batter into the prepared pans and bake for 30 to 40 minutes or until the cake springs back when pressed lightly in the center.

CHOCOLATE CAKE

Yellow Cake Recipe

2 T. milk

2 squares unsweetened baker's chocolate

Follow the directions for Yellow Cake recipe with the following differences:

Add milk and melted baker's chocolate. If you don't have baking chocolate, you can substitute semisweet chocolate chips or 5 to 6 tablespoons of unsweetened cocoa powder.

SPICE CAKE

Yellow Cake Recipe

1 tsp. ground cinnamon

½ tsp. allspice

½ tsp. ground cloves

Follow the directions for Yellow Cake recipe with the following differences:

Right after pouring the cake mix into a two-quart bowl, stir in ground cinnamon, allspice, and ground cloves, then continue with the directions.

MASTER CHOCOLATE PUDDING MIX

4 cups nonfat instant dry milk

2⅔ cups cornstarch

1¼ cups unsweetened cocoa powder

½ tsp. salt

Mix all ingredients until very well blended. Store in an airtight container.

CHOCOLATE PUDDING

In a heavy-bottomed saucepan, mix together the pudding mix and milk, whisking vigorously to blend well. Over medium heat, bring to a low boil while stirring constantly and boil just until pudding thickens a bit. (The pudding thickens more as it cools.) Remove from heat and stir in the butter and vanilla. Pour into individual bowls and cool.

I don't always add butter because I like the mouthfeel better that way. If you think that could be the case for you, try adding half that amount and go from there.

1 cup Master Chocolate Pudding Mix

2 cups milk

1 T. butter

½ tsp. vanilla

MASTER CORN BREAD MIX

4 cups flour

1½ cups instant nonfat dry milk

1 T. salt

¾ cup sugar

¼ cup baking powder

1 cup shortening

4½ cups cornmeal

In a large mixing bowl, combine the flour, dry milk, salt, sugar, and baking powder and mix well. Add the shortening and work with a pastry cutter or two forks until the shortening has been well incorporated and the mixture resembles coarse cornmeal. Add the cornmeal and mix well again.

Place in an airtight container or large plastic storage bag and store in a cool, dark place. Date the container and use within three to four months.

CORN BREAD WITH HONEY BUTTER

To make corn bread:

Preheat the oven to 400°. Grease or butter an 8 × 8-inch baking dish; set aside for now.

In a small bowl, combine the egg and water; beat well by hand, using a fork to help break up and disperse the egg. In a medium mixing bowl, add the Master Corn Bread Mix. Make a well in the center and add the egg mixture all at once. Stir just until blended.

Pour batter into the prepared baking dish and bake for 25 to 30 minutes. When ready to eat, spread with Honey Butter.

To make honey butter:

Using an electric mixer or handheld eggbeater, blend together until light and fluffy. (It takes me about 5 minutes when I'm using my handheld beater.) Store in the refrigerator if possible.

Corn Bread:

1 egg, beaten

1¼ cups water

2¾ cups Master Corn Bread Mix

Honey Butter:

1 cup butter, softened

1½ cups honey

CORN MUFFINS

Follow the recipe above for Corn Bread, with these differences:

Preheat the oven to 425°.

Grease a muffin pan or line the cups with paper cupcake liners. Fill the muffin cups two-thirds full and bake for 15 to 20 minutes.

Corn Bread Recipe

MASTER CREAM OF CHICKEN SOUP MIX

2 cups instant
nonfat dry milk

¾ cup cornstarch

¼ cup chicken
bouillon granules

1 tsp. salt

½ tsp. black pepper

½ tsp. onion powder

Whisk together all ingredients until well blended; store in a quart jar with tight-fitting lid or a quart ziplock bag.

CREAM OF CHICKEN SOUP

1¼ cups water

⅓ cup Master
Cream of Chicken
Soup Mix

In a medium saucepan, whisk together the water and soup mix. Bring to a simmer, stirring constantly, and boil until the soup thickens.

MASTER "GRAHAM NUTS" CEREAL

3½ cups whole
wheat flour

1 cup brown sugar

1 tsp. salt

1 tsp. baking soda

1 tsp. ground
cinnamon

2 cups buttermilk

2 tsp. vanilla

Preheat the oven to 350°.

In a large bowl, combine all ingredients and mix well. Pour out onto an oiled 12 × 16-inch low-sided baking pan and spread evenly with a spatula. Bake for about 20 minutes or until the batter is firm, medium brown in color, and has begun to shrink away slightly from the sides of the pan. Remove the pan from the oven and turn off the heat. With a metal spatula, completely loosen the hot patty and transfer the patty to a rack to cool for several hours. If the patty breaks, don't worry—just lay the pieces on the rack to cool.

When the patty has fully cooled, preheat the oven to 275°.

Break the patty into chunks and put it through a meat grinder or a food processor until coarse crumbs are formed. Divide the crumbs between two 12 × 16-inch low-sided pans.

Bake for 30 to 40 minutes, stirring every 10 minutes, until the crumbs seem dry. Let cool and then store in an airtight container.

Note: Our family has eaten this cereal for a good 40 years—we love the stuff! We eat it plain as a snack, with milk as a cold cereal, and as a topping on yogurt, ice cream, and homemade tapioca pudding.

MASTER GRANOLA MIX

2 cups whole
wheat flour

6 cups rolled oats

1 cup dried,
shredded coconut

1 cup wheat germ
(or another cup of
whole wheat flour)

1 T. salt

½ cup water

1 cup neutral oil,
such as vegetable
or canola

1 cup honey

2 tsp. vanilla

Preheat the oven to 250°. Lightly grease two large cookie sheets and set aside.

In your largest mixing bowl, mix all dry ingredients until thoroughly combined.

In a medium bowl, whisk the liquid ingredients until well blended. Pour the liquid into the large bowl of dry ingredients and mix thoroughly. Spread the granola out on the two cookie sheets and bake for 1 hour or until dry and golden. Halfway through cooking time, gently turn the granola on the cookie sheets so it dries evenly.

Cool completely and then store in a covered container.

Variations: Use maple syrup instead of honey; leave out the coconut; after baking, add chopped nuts such as sliced almonds, chopped pecans, or walnut pieces. You can also add pieces of dehydrated fruit after baking, such as blueberries, apples, raisins, bananas, or strawberries.

MASTER HOT CHOCOLATE MIX I

6½ cups instant nonfat dry milk

1 cup powdered sugar

1 cup granulated sugar

1 cup unsweetened baking cocoa

Dash of salt

In a large mixing bowl, combine all ingredients and mix well. Place in an airtight container or large plastic storage bag. Store in a cool, dry place and use within six months.

HOT CHOCOLATE BY THE CUP

Pour the hot water or milk into a mug and then stir in the Hot Chocolate Mix.

1 cup very hot water or milk

3 T. Master Hot Chocolate Mix I

MASTER HOT CHOCOLATE MIX II

10⅔ cups instant nonfat dry milk

1 (6-oz.) jar powdered nondairy creamer

2 cups powdered sugar

1 (16-oz.) can instant chocolate drink mix

In a large bowl, combine all ingredients and mix very well. Place in an airtight container or large storage bag. Store in a cool, dry place and use within six months.

HOT CHOCOLATE BY THE CUP

1 cup very hot water

3 T. Master Hot Chocolate Mix II

Pour the hot water into a mug and then stir in the Hot Chocolate Mix.

MASTER "INSTANT" OATMEAL

6 cups quick cooking rolled oats

⅓ cup brown sugar

2 tsp. cinnamon

¾ to 1 tsp. salt

Note: Make this recipe ahead of time so on busy mornings, when time is at a premium, this "fast food" will provide a healthy breakfast for you and your family.

Preheat the oven to 325°. Spread the oats on a baking sheet (you may need to do this in two batches, depending on the size of your baking sheet). Bake for 20 minutes. Cool completely.

Combine 4 cups of the oats, brown sugar, cinnamon, and salt in a food processor and pulse just until you achieve a rough powder (there will still be bits of oats). Mix the remaining 2 cups of oats into the pulsed oats and mix well to thoroughly combine.

Place the oatmeal in a large container with a tight-fitting lid and store in the pantry or a cupboard, where it will stay fresh for several months—no need to refrigerate.

INSTANT OATMEAL

Place ½ cup of the Master "Instant" Oatmeal mixture in a bowl and pour in about 1 cup of boiling water (you can use a bit more if you like your oatmeal thinner). Stir and then cover the bowl with a plate. Let the oatmeal sit for about 4 to 5 minutes; stir again and serve.

You can add some warm milk (consider using less boiling water if you choose to add milk), fruit, nuts, seeds, and/or raisins to the oatmeal.

MASTER OATMEAL MUFFIN MIX

3 cups flour

1 cup instant nonfat dry milk

3½ tsp. baking powder

1½ tsp. salt

½ cup granulated sugar

1 cup brown sugar

1½ cups shortening

3 cups rolled oats

In a large mixing bowl, sift together the flour, dry milk, baking powder, salt, and granulated sugar. Mix well; add the brown sugar and mix well again. Add the shortening and work with a pastry cutter or two forks until shortening has been well incorporated and the mixture resembles coarse cornmeal. Stir in oats and mix well again. Place in an airtight container or large plastic storage bag. Store in a cool, dry place. Date the container and use within three to four months.

Note: This is one of our go-to mixes, so I usually make a double batch because it goes quickly!

OATMEAL MUFFINS

1 egg

⅔ cup water or milk

3 cups Master Oatmeal Muffin Mix

Preheat the oven to 400°.

In a small bowl, mix the egg and water or milk; beat well by hand, using a fork to help break up and disperse the egg. Measure the Master Oatmeal Muffin Mix into a medium mixing bowl and make a well in the middle. Add the egg mixture all at once and mix by hand just until the dry ingredients are moistened—the batter will be lumpy. Fill greased muffin cups two-thirds full and bake for 15 to 20 minutes or until tops are golden brown.

Variations: Add some fresh, frozen, dried, or canned and drained blueberries; before baking, sprinkle the tops with some sugar or cinnamon sugar.

MASTER ONION SOUP MIX

¼ cup dehydrated onion flakes

2 T. beef bouillon granules

¼ tsp. onion powder

¼ tsp. parsley flakes

⅛ tsp. paprika

⅛ tsp. black pepper

The following directions are for making individual packets versus one large batch. This way, each packet will have consistent ingredients and, therefore, flavor.

Combine all ingredients until very well mixed. For each packet, place the mixed ingredients onto a 6-inch square of aluminum foil and fold to make airtight. You can make a number of these packets at one time—just place all the packets into a plastic storage bag and use within six months.

ONION SOUP

In a medium saucepan, bring the water to a simmer; whisk in the soup mix, reduce the heat a bit, and simmer, stirring occasionally, for 5 minutes.

3½ cups water

1 packet Master Onion Soup Mix

MASTER PANCAKE MIX

10 cups flour

2½ cups instant nonfat dry milk

½ cup sugar

¼ cup baking powder

2 T. salt

Combine all ingredients in a large bowl and mix well. Place in an airtight container or large plastic storage bags. Store in a cool, dry place and use within eight months.

BASIC PANCAKES

1 egg, beaten

1 cup water

3 T. vegetable oil

1½ cups Master Pancake Mix

In a small bowl, mix the egg and water; beat well by hand, using a fork to help break up and disperse the egg. Beat in the vegetable oil. Measure the Master Pancake Mix into a medium mixing bowl and add the egg mixture; mix well. If the batter seems too thick, add a bit more water and stir well again.

Let the pancake batter stand for 5 minutes and then cook the pancakes, turning once, until golden on both sides.

MASTER RANCH DRESSING AND DIP MIX

2 tsp. instant minced onion

½ tsp. salt

⅛ tsp. garlic powder

2 T. dried parsley flakes

2 T. buttermilk powder

If you're anything like our family, having ranch dressing available at all times is practically a must, because everything tastes better with ranch! This is also best to make as individual packets.

Combine all ingredients until very well mixed. For each packet, place the mixed ingredients onto a 6-inch square of aluminum foil and fold to make airtight. You can make a number of these packets at one time—just place all the packets into a plastic storage bag and use within six months.

RANCH DIP

Combine all ingredients in a quart jar and shake until well blended. Chill before serving.

1 packet Master Ranch Dressing and Dip Mix

1 cup mayonnaise

1 cup sour cream

SALAD DRESSING

Combine all ingredients in a quart jar and shake until well blended. Chill before serving.

1 packet Master Ranch Dressing and Dip Mix

1 cup mayonnaise

¾ cup water

MASTER CHEESY SCALLOPED POTATO SAUCE MIX

½ cup flour

½ cup cornstarch

¾ cup cheddar cheese powder

1 cup instant nonfat dry milk

⅛ cup dehydrated onions

1 tsp. onion powder

1 tsp. salt

1 T. chicken bouillon granules

2 tsp. ground mustard

1 tsp. garlic powder

1 tsp. black pepper

18 cups dehydrated sliced potatoes

Whisk together all ingredients except the potatoes. Store the dry sauce mix in a quart jar with a tight-fitting lid or ziplock quart bag.

Store the potatoes separately in a gallon jar or ziplock bag; there will be slightly more than a gallon of potatoes, so store the excess in a quart jar or bag and use those first.

CHEESY SCALLOPED POTATOES

½ cup Master Cheesy Scalloped Potato Sauce Mix

2¾ cups boiling water

2 T. butter or butter powder

3 cups dehydrated sliced potatoes

Whisk sauce mix with the boiling water and butter. Pour into a greased or buttered 9 × 13-inch baking pan. Add the potatoes, pushing them down under the sauce. Cover and let the potatoes sit while the oven is preheating to 350°. Bake, covered, for 30 minutes. Uncover, and bake for an additional 15 minutes or until done.

MASTER STOVETOP STUFFING MIX

6 cups cubed bread

1 T. dried parsley

3 T. chicken or beef bouillon granules

¼ cup dehydrated minced onion

½ cup dehydrated minced celery

1 tsp. thyme

1 tsp. pepper

½ tsp. sage (can omit if using beef bouillon)

½ tsp. salt

Preheat the oven to 350°. Spread the bread cubes in one layer on a large baking sheet. Bake for 8 to 10 minutes; allow to cool completely. Mix the bread cubes with the rest of the ingredients and store in a half-gallon jar or gallon ziplock bag.

STOVETOP STUFFING

In a medium saucepan, bring the water and butter to a gentle boil, making sure the butter has completely melted. Turn off the heat but leave the saucepan on the heated element and immediately add the stuffing mix. Stir with a fork, cover the pot, and let the stuffing rest for several minutes. Fluff and serve.

¾ cup water

2 to 3 T. butter

2 cups Master Stovetop Stuffing Mix

MASTER TACO SEASONING MIX

½ cup (heaping) chili powder

3 T. ground cumin

1 T. salt

1 T. black pepper

1 T. sweet paprika

2 tsp. garlic

2 tsp. onion powder

2 tsp. oregano

1 to 2 tsp. crushed red pepper flakes

Master Taco Seasoning Mix is also a great seasoning for chili, soup, and stew.

The pepper flakes are optional if you like hot taco seasoning. Put all ingredients into a pint canning jar that has a tight-fitting lid or other suitable container or baggie. Roll the jar or gently shake the bag until all ingredients are well mixed, and roll or shake each time you use it, as the ingredients can settle.

TACO MEAT

1 lb. hamburger

2 to 2½ T. Master Taco Seasoning Mix

¼ cup water

Brown hamburger; drain off fat. Return to heat and add the seasoning and water. Bring to a simmer and cook until liquid has thickened, about 2 minutes.

MASTER BASIC SEASONED TOMATO SAUCE

½ cup extra virgin olive oil

1 large yellow onion, diced

Salt to taste

1 head garlic, crushed to remove outer paper from cloves, and then thinly sliced or minced

1 carrot, peeled and finely shredded

1½ T. dried thyme

1 wine glass red wine (optional)

1 #10 can (106 oz.) crushed tomatoes

This is another recipe my brother developed, and it is another taste winner!

In a large pot, heat olive oil over medium-high heat until shimmering. Add the onion with a generous pinch of salt and sweat the onion, stirring frequently for 6 to 8 minutes. Add garlic and carrot with another pinch of salt and continue to sauté for another 5 minutes or until the carrot is soft and the onion is beginning to caramelize. Add the thyme and wine (if using) and sauté, stirring occasionally, for another several minutes. Pour in the crushed tomatoes, reduce heat to medium, and bring to a simmer, stirring frequently and keeping the pot partially or fully covered. Simmer for 30 minutes, stirring occasionally. Remove from heat, adjust salt to taste, and allow to cool before freezing or using.

To freeze, measure out tomato sauce in 2-cup containers with tight-fitting lids, and freeze for up to several months.

This sauce is best thawed in the refrigerator.

Examples for use:

- Use as is, or add sautéed mushrooms and bring to a simmer to heat up and meld flavors.
- Sauté some crushed red pepper flakes in a bit of olive oil. Stir in the tomato sauce and heat through. This is excellent mixed with cooked pasta.

MASTER WHITE SAUCE AND GRAVY MIX

2 cups instant nonfat dry milk

1 cup flour

2 tsp. salt

1 cup very cold butter

In a large mixing bowl, combine the dry milk, flour, and salt. Mix well. Cut the cold butter into small pieces and work with a pastry cutter or two forks to cut the butter into the flour mix until the butter has been well incorporated and the mixture resembles coarse cornmeal. Lightly pack into an airtight container or plastic storage bag. Store in the refrigerator or an equivalent cold area, such as an unheated basement. Date the container and use within the "best by" date of the butter.

BASIC WHITE SAUCE

¼ to ½ cup Master White Sauce and Gravy Mix

1 cup cold water or milk

Salt and pepper to taste

Use more or less sauce mix depending on how thin you want the finished sauce to be. In a small saucepan, combine the sauce mix with the water or milk. Cook over low heat, stirring constantly, until smooth and thickened. Season with salt and pepper.

CHEESE SAUCE

Follow the recipe for Basic White Sauce. When the sauce has thickened, add cheese and then season to taste.

Basic White Sauce Recipe

3/4 cup grated cheddar or Parmesan cheese

Seasonings to taste

BEEF OR CHICKEN GRAVY

Use more or less sauce mix, depending on how thin you want the finished sauce to be. In a small saucepan, combine the sauce mix with your choice of broth. Cook, stirring constantly, over low heat, until smooth and thickened. Season to taste.

¼ to ½ cup Master White Sauce and Gravy Mix

1 cup beef or chicken broth

Seasonings of choice, such as salt, pepper, Worcestershire sauce, garlic powder, or herbs

BREAD, MUFFINS, ROLLS, AND CRACKERS

In this chapter, you'll find recipes for bread, muffins, rolls, crackers, and so much more. We'll start off with Cornell's formula for adding extra protein to homemade bread. Developed in the 1930s by a professor at Cornell University, you can use this formula in either white or wheat bread, and it will actually enhance the flavor of your finished product.

CORNELL UNIVERSITY'S TRIPLE-RICH PROTEIN FORMULA

1 T. soy flour

1 T. dry milk powder

1 tsp. wheat germ

For every cup measure of flour in a baking recipe, first put all these ingredients into the bottom of the cup and then fill it to the top with your flour. Continue as directed in the recipe.

BACON AND CHEDDAR CHEESE MUFFINS

2 cups flour

2 T. sugar

3 tsp. baking powder

½ tsp. salt

½ cup cooked, crumbled bacon

½ cup cheddar cheese

¼ cup finely diced sweet onion (optional)

1 cup milk

1 egg, beaten

4 T. butter, melted and cooled to lukewarm

Preheat the oven to 425°. Grease a muffin pan or line with paper cupcake liners.

In a large bowl, mix the flour, sugar, baking powder, and salt. Add the bacon, cheese, and onion (if using) and mix again. Make a well in the center of the flour mixture.

In a small bowl, mix the milk, egg, and butter. Mix well; pour mixture all at once into the well and stir just until moistened. Batter will be lumpy.

Fill the prepared muffin cups about two-thirds full and bake for 20 to 25 minutes. Immediately remove muffins from pan and place on rack to cool.

BAGELS

In a large mixing bowl, combine 1½ cups of the flour with the yeast.

In a separate bowl, combine the water, sugar, and salt and then add this to the flour mixture. Beat at low speed for about 30 seconds, scraping the side of the bowl constantly. Beat for 3 minutes on high speed.

Stir in as much of the remaining flour as you can and then turn it out onto a lightly floured surface. Knead while continuing to add enough flour to make a moderately stiff dough. Continue kneading until smooth and elastic. Cover and allow to rest for 15 minutes.

Cut dough into 12 portions and shape each into a smooth ball. Punch a hole in the middle of each with a floured finger. Pull gently to enlarge the hole to about 2 inches across.

Place the bagels on a greased baking sheet, cover, and let rise for 20 minutes.

Preheat the oven to 350°.

Bring a large kettle of water to a gentle boil, place the bagels in the boiling water for about 10 to 15 seconds, and then remove and allow to drain for a moment before placing them on a greased baking sheet.

Bake 8 to 10 minutes, and then broil them for about 90 seconds on each side to brown.

4½ cups flour, more or less, divided

4½ tsp. (2 packets) active dry yeast

1½ cups warm water (about 110°)

3 T. sugar

1 T. salt

BASIC PER LOAF BREAD

For each loaf of bread:

1 cup warm water, about 110° (or use half water and half milk)

1 tsp. melted shortening, butter, or vegetable oil

1 scant tsp. salt

2 T. honey, sugar, or liquid sweetener of your choice

1 tsp. active dry yeast

3 cups flour

Note: If you want to make more than one loaf at a time, you can simply double or even triple the ingredients, but note that if you decide to make four loaves at one time, you'll adjust the amount of yeast and only use one rounded tablespoon.

In a mixing bowl, stir together the water, fat, salt, and sweetener. Sprinkle yeast over the top of the mixture and let it stand until the yeast dissolves and starts bubbling, about 10 minutes.

Stir in half of the total amount of flour you plan on using (for instance, 1½ cups flour for each loaf) and beat until smooth. You can use an electric mixer for this part if desired, but you can also mix by hand using a large wooden spoon. Add enough of the remaining flour to make a dough ball that holds together and comes away from the sides of the bowl.

Place the dough onto a floured surface and knead for 5 to 10 minutes, adding more flour as needed to keep from sticking.

Put the dough into a large, greased bowl and grease the surfaces of the dough as well. Cover with a towel and let rise until doubled. Punch down and then lightly knead the dough for a minute or so, grease the surfaces of the dough again, and let it rise in the greased bowl a second time until doubled. Punch down the dough and form into a loaf. (If you are making multiple loaves, cut or tear the dough into the required number of pieces before continuing.) Place the loaf seam side down into a greased loaf pan and let it rise until almost doubled, usually about 1 inch over the top of the loaf pan.

Preheat the oven to 400°. Place the loaf in the preheated oven and immediately turn the heat down to 350°. Bake about 30 minutes or until done. Remove the loaf from the oven, grease or butter the top of the bread if desired, and then take it out of the pan and cool on a wire rack.

BERRY MUFFINS

Preheat the oven to 375°. Grease a muffin tin or line the cups with paper cupcake liners.

In a large bowl, stir together the flour, 1 cup sugar, baking powder, cinnamon, and salt.

In another bowl, stir together milk, butter, egg, and vanilla. Add to the dry ingredients and stir just until blended. Batter will be lumpy. Fold in berries.

Fill prepared muffin cups three-fourths full. Sprinkle with remaining sugar. Bake 20 minutes or until done.

1¾ cups flour

1 cup plus 1 T. sugar, divided

2½ tsp. baking powder

½ tsp. cinnamon

¼ tsp. salt

1 cup milk

¼ cup butter, melted and cooled to lukewarm

1 egg, beaten

1 tsp. vanilla

1 cup berries, fresh or frozen (blueberries, blackberries, and raspberries are a great combination)

BLUEBERRY OATMEAL MUFFINS

1 cup flour

2 tsp. baking powder

½ tsp. salt

½ tsp. cinnamon

½ cup brown sugar

¾ cup rolled oats

1 egg

1 cup milk

¼ cup butter, melted and cooled to lukewarm

¾ cup blueberries, fresh or frozen

Sugar or cinnamon sugar for sprinkling

Preheat the oven to 375°. Grease a 12-cup muffin tin and set aside for now.

In a medium bowl, stir together the flour, baking powder, salt, and cinnamon. Add the sugar and oats and mix well.

In a large mixing bowl, beat together the egg, milk, and butter. Add the dry ingredients and stir just until moistened. Fold in blueberries.

Fill prepared muffin cups two-thirds full. Sprinkle the tops with sugar or cinnamon sugar. Bake for 20 minutes or until done.

CINNAMON FANS

Preheat the oven to 400°. Grease a 12-cup muffin tin and set aside for now.

Make the dough: Stir together dry ingredients. Cut in shortening until the mixture resembles coarse crumbs. Add milk and stir. On a floured surface, knead dough gently for half a minute. Roll dough into the shape of a rectangle about ¼-inch thick. (The rectangle should be about 8 × 24 inches.)

Make the filling: Spread the filling ingredients over the top of the dough, starting with the butter and then sprinkling the sugar and cinnamon over the butter. Cut the dough the long way into four 2-inch-wide strips. Stack the strips on top of one another and cut the stack into 2-inch-wide strip pieces. Turn the pieces on their sides in the prepared muffin cups so each treat fans out.

Bake for 12 minutes or until golden brown.

For the dough:

3 cups flour

1 tsp. salt

4 tsp. baking powder

1 tsp. cream of tartar

⅓ cup sugar

¾ cup shortening

1 cup milk

For the filling:

½ cup butter, melted and cooled

½ cup sugar

2 T. cinnamon

EASY CINNAMON ROLLS

Cinnamon Rolls:

¾ cup milk

¾ cup water

½ cup shortening

½ cup sugar

2 eggs

2 tsp. salt

4½ tsp. (2 packets) active dry yeast, dissolved in ½ cup warm water (110°)

7 cups flour, more or less

½ cup butter, melted

Cinnamon and sugar mixture

Sugar Glaze (optional):

1½ cups powdered sugar

2 to 3 T. water

To make the cinnamon rolls: On the stovetop, heat the milk and water together until scalded. Cool to lukewarm.

In a large mixing bowl, mix the shortening, sugar, eggs, and salt. (You can use an electric mixer for this.) Add the milk mixture and stir well. Add dissolved yeast and stir well again. Add enough of the flour so the dough pulls away from the sides of the bowl. Turn out dough ball onto a floured surface and add the remaining flour as needed to keep dough from sticking as you knead for 5 minutes.

Place dough in a large, greased bowl, turning dough ball so entire surface is greased. Cover with a towel and let rise until doubled in bulk, about 1 hour. While the dough is rising, add melted butter to a shallow bowl and place the cinnamon sugar in another shallow bowl.

Roll dough out to ¼-inch thickness. Cut with a biscuit cutter. Roll each piece so it's long and thin. Dip each piece in the melted butter and then dredge in the cinnamon sugar. Roll each piece up and place each one on baking sheets with sides not quite touching. Let rise about 30 to 45 minutes.

When the rolls are almost finished rising, preheat the oven to 350°. Bake for 15 minutes or until done.

To make the sugar glaze: Mix the powdered sugar and water until well blended and a desired consistency. Drizzle or spread over cooled cinnamon rolls.

ENGLISH MUFFINS

In a large bowl, mix the milk and yeast. Let this sit for 10 minutes or until the yeast is bubbly.

Add the butter, salt, sugar, egg, and flour and mix by hand or with an electric mixer for 5 minutes—the dough will be very soft and sticky.

Scrape the dough out into another large bowl that has been greased (you can use shortening, oil, or butter) and cover with a clean towel. Let the dough rise for 2 hours.

Grease your hands and pinch off small pieces of dough. Form each piece into a ball and place them on a large baking sheet that has been generously sprinkled with cornmeal or covered with greased parchment paper. Flatten the balls by gently pressing down on the tops. Let them rest for 20 minutes.

Preheat a griddle or heavy pan (cast iron works well) on a medium-low setting. Carefully transfer the English muffins to the preheated griddle, making sure not to crowd them in the pan, and cook until the bottoms are a deep golden brown. Flip the English muffins and continue to cook them until that side is deep golden brown also.

Transfer the cooked English muffins to a rack to cool completely before serving. Use a fork to split them open.

1¾ cups warm milk (about 110° to 115°)

2¼ tsp. (1 packet) active dry yeast

3 T. butter, softened

1¼ tsp. salt

2 T. sugar

1 egg

4½ cups flour

Cornmeal for sprinkling

FLOUR TORTILLAS

2 cups flour

1 tsp. baking powder

½ tsp. salt

5 T. shortening or lard

¾ cup hot water

In a large bowl, combine the flour, baking powder, and salt. Add the fat and mix using a pastry cutter or your fingers until the mixture resembles pea-sized crumbles. Add the hot water and continue to mix, using a wooden spoon, until dough forms.

Turn the dough out onto a lightly floured surface and knead about 15 times, adding a bit more water or flour if needed to create a smooth dough. Cover with a damp towel; let the dough rest for 10 minutes.

Divide the dough into 12 equal portions; cover and let the dough balls rest again for another 10 minutes.

Roll each ball into a circle about 7 inches across or however thick or thin you desire.

Heat a dry skillet or griddle over medium-high heat and cook each tortilla until brown blisters begin to form and the dough is cooked through, about 1 minute per side.

Serve them immediately or cool and store them in a ziplock bag in the refrigerator for 3 to 5 days.

FRENCH BREAD

Note: French bread can't be hurried. The ingredients are minimal, but it's the process that gives French bread its spectacular taste and texture. Start this bread early in the day and it will be ready for dinner. And do plan to eat it all in one sitting because French bread doesn't store well.

1 T. active dry yeast

¼ cup warm water (110°)

½ tsp. sugar

2 cups lukewarm water

2 tsp. salt

6 cups flour, divided

Small amount of cornmeal

In a small bowl, mix the yeast, ¼ cup warm water, and sugar. Let sit until the yeast is dissolved and the mixture begins to bubble and rise.

In a large bowl, mix the 2 cups lukewarm water and salt. Add the dissolved yeast mixture and stir well. Using an electric mixer, add 2 cups flour and beat on low speed for 1 minute. Increase speed to medium and beat for another 2 minutes. Scrape the sides of the bowl regularly to get all the bits of flour into the batter.

By hand, stir in enough of the remaining flour to make a ball of dough that pulls away from the sides of the bowl. It will be very soft and sticky.

If the dough seems too sticky to successfully turn out and knead, keep it in the bowl for now and knead the dough with a large wooden spoon or paddle, adding small amounts of flour as you work. After kneading the dough for several minutes, the dough will not be as sticky, and you can then turn the dough ball out onto a well-floured surface or on a floured pastry cloth. The dough will still be somewhat sticky but do your best to work around that.

Knead the dough for about 8 minutes or until it is shiny, elastic, and has air bubbles under the surface. Don't rush this step. Place the dough ball in a very large, greased bowl and turn the ball of dough so all surfaces are greased. Cover the bowl with a towel and let the dough rise until it's tripled in volume. This will easily take 3 or more hours. Again, you don't want to hurry this rise time because the slow rising will enhance the flavor and texture of the finished loaves.

After the dough has risen, turn it out again on a floured surface and gently knead for several minutes to get out the air bubbles—use a toothpick if necessary. Place the dough back in the greased bowl, turning to grease all surfaces, and let it rise a second time until it's slightly more than doubled. This second rising will take less time, but it will still take at least an hour.

Turn out the dough once more onto the floured surface and gently knead for 2 minutes, making sure to prick the bubbles with a toothpick. Using your hands, flatten the dough into a rectangle and cut into 3 equal portions. Cover them with a towel and let rest for 15 minutes. Then form each portion into a long, narrow loaf by rolling the dough back and forth with your hands and pricking out air bubbles with a toothpick. Make the loaves almost as long as the cookie sheet you will use for baking.

Grease a large cookie sheet and then liberally sprinkle cornmeal on it. Carefully lay the loaves on the cookie sheet, cover with a towel, and let rise again until almost tripled in bulk, about 45 to 60 minutes.

Place a shallow pan of boiling water on the floor of the oven and preheat the oven to 400°. Just before baking, diagonally slash the tops of the loaves in several places using a very sharp knife, and then mist or brush the loaves with cold water. You can also sprinkle on sesame or poppy seeds if desired.

Bake 25 to 35 minutes or until done, misting the bread occasionally while it bakes.

GARLIC CHEESE BREADSTICKS

Preheat the oven to 450°.

Pour butter into a 9 × 13-inch baking pan. In a mixing bowl, mix the flour, baking powder, and milk and stir until a soft dough forms. Knead about 3 minutes, adding extra flour if the dough is too sticky.

Roll out dough to form two 8-inch squares. Cut each square in half and then cut into 4 × 1½-inch strips (6 strips from each half square). Place the strips into the pan and turn them so both sides are buttered. Sprinkle the strips with garlic powder, Parmesan cheese, and optional parsley.

Bake for 15 to 20 minutes or until done and golden in color.

½ cup butter, melted

2½ cups flour

4 tsp. baking powder

1⅓ cups milk

2 tsp. garlic powder

Parmesan cheese to taste

Dried parsley (optional)

GRAHAM CRACKERS

Preheat the oven to 375°. Lightly grease a cookie sheet or use a silicone baking mat.

Mix all ingredients except for the cinnamon sugar. Turn the dough out onto the prepared cookie sheet and roll out thinly and evenly. Sprinkle the surface with cinnamon sugar and lightly press sugar mixture into the surface of dough. Deeply score dough in squares (a pizza cutter works well).

Bake for about 8 minutes or until done. (The time might vary depending on how thick or thin the crackers are.) Allow to cool slightly before cutting through the crackers.

2 cups whole wheat flour

2 tsp. baking powder

¼ tsp. salt

4 T. brown sugar

½ cup butter

2 T. honey

2 T. milk

Dash of vanilla

Cinnamon sugar for sprinkling

KNEE PATCHES

3 eggs

1 tsp. vanilla

2 tsp. salt

1 cup heavy cream

4 cups flour

Vegetable oil for frying

Powdered sugar for sprinkling (optional)

Cinnamon sugar for sprinkling (optional)

Note: Knee Patches are also known as Elephant Ears.

In a large mixing bowl, beat the eggs until frothy. Add the vanilla, salt, and cream and mix until well blended. Gradually add the flour and beat thoroughly. Because the dough will be stiff, consider using a large wooden spoon. Turn out dough onto a floured surface and knead for 10 minutes.

Preheat about 2 quarts oil to 375° in a deep-fat fryer or deep cast-iron pot. Pinch off small pieces of dough about the size of an unshelled walnut and roll out to shape a 4-inch circle. Now comes the fun part! Sit down and cover one of your knees with a clean towel. Lay the rolled-out dough on the towel and stretch the dough over your kneecap, working the dough until it's very thin.

Deep fry the knee patches in the hot oil for about 2 minutes per side. The knee patches will puff as they cook. Remove them carefully from the oil and lay them on paper towels to drain. Sprinkle the knee patches with powdered sugar or cinnamon sugar if using and eat while warm and fresh.

MASHED POTATO ROLLS

In a large bowl, dissolve yeast in warm water. Add milk, butter, oil, sugar, egg, and mashed potatoes and mix well. Stir in salt, baking powder, baking soda, and half the flour. Mix either by hand or using a stand mixer, adding the rest of the flour until a soft dough is formed.

Turn out onto a floured surface and knead 6 to 8 minutes or until the dough is smooth and elastic.

Place the dough in a large, greased bowl and turn so the entire surface of the dough is greased. Cover with a clean towel and let rise until doubled, about 1½ hours.

Punch down dough. Turn out onto a lightly floured surface and shape bits of dough into approximately 32 round balls. Place balls 2 inches apart on greased baking sheets. Cover and let rise until doubled, about 45 minutes.

Bake in a preheated 375° oven 15 to 18 minutes or until done and golden. Remove from the oven and, if desired, immediately brush or dip tops of rolls in melted butter. Set on racks to cool.

Note: If you don't have any leftover mashed potatoes and you're in a hurry, you can use dehydrated mashed potatoes. Just mix according to the package directions and use in place of fresh mashed potatoes.

2¼ tsp. (1 packet) active dry yeast

¼ cup warm water (110°)

1¾ cups warm milk (110°)

¼ cup butter, room temperature

¼ cup oil

6 T. sugar

1 egg

½ cup mashed potatoes

1½ tsp. salt

1 tsp. baking powder

½ tsp. baking soda

6 cups flour, divided

Melted butter (optional)

ONE-HOUR BUTTERMILK ROLLS

4½ tsp. (2 packets) yeast

¼ cup warm water (110°)

3 T. sugar

½ cup shortening, melted and cooled slightly

1½ cups buttermilk, heated to lukewarm

4½ cups flour

½ tsp. baking soda

1 tsp. salt

In a large mixing bowl or the bowl of a stand mixer, dissolve the yeast in the water. When the yeast has dissolved and is bubbly, add the sugar and shortening and blend on low speed to mix. Add the remaining ingredients and beat until smooth. Let the dough rise for 10 minutes, and then shape into rolls and set them on a greased baking sheet. Let the rolls rise for 30 minutes more.

Preheat the oven to 400°. Bake for 15 to 20 minutes or until the rolls are golden colored and done.

OVERNIGHT NO-KNEAD BUTTER ROLLS

In a small bowl, sprinkle the yeast over ¼ cup of the warm water and let sit until it begins to froth and bubble, about 10 minutes.

In a large mixing bowl, beat the eggs and then stir in the yeast mixture. Add 2½ cups of the flour, alternating with the remaining warm water. Add the sugar, ½ cup of the melted butter, and the salt and mix until smooth. Beat in the remaining flour to make a soft dough. Cover with a towel and let rise until doubled, about 1½ to 2 hours. Punch down dough, cover with plastic wrap, and refrigerate overnight.

The next day, remove the dough from the refrigerator and set on counter to warm up a bit, 30 to 45 minutes. Grease 2 muffin tins and set aside for now.

Punch down the dough and divide it in half. On a floured surface, roll out each half into an 8 × 15-inch rectangle.

Spread with lots of softened butter. Starting with a long edge, roll up dough jelly-roll style. With a very sharp knife, cut into 1¼-inch-thick slices. Place slices in the prepared muffin tin cups, cut side up. Cover and let rise until doubled, about 1 hour.

Preheat the oven to 400°.

Bake the rolls for 8 to 10 minutes or until rolls are golden brown. Immediately upon removing from the oven, brush tops with the remaining melted butter. Remove from muffin tins and cool on a wire rack.

4½ tsp. (2 packets) yeast

1¼ cups warm water (110°), divided

3 eggs

5 cups flour, divided

½ cup sugar

¾ cup melted butter, divided

2 tsp. salt

At least ½ cup softened butter for spreading

PEACH MUFFINS (WITH CANNED PEACHES)

Muffins:

1¼ cups flour

1½ tsp. baking powder

½ tsp. salt

⅔ cup sugar

1 cup canned peaches, drained and chopped, divided

½ cup milk

1 egg

¼ cup vegetable oil

1 tsp. vanilla

Streusel Topping:

¼ cup flour

3 T. sugar

½ tsp. baking powder

½ tsp. cinnamon

4 T. cold butter, cut into pieces

To make muffins:

Preheat the oven to 350°. Grease the cups of a muffin tin or use paper cupcake liners.

In a large mixing bowl, whisk together the flour, baking powder, salt, and sugar. Add ¾ cup of the peaches and stir well to coat. Next, add the milk, egg, oil, and vanilla and stir just until the flour is moistened.

Fill the prepared muffin cups three-fourths full.

To make streusel topping:

In a small bowl, combine the flour, sugar, baking powder, and cinnamon and stir to mix. Add the butter and mix, breaking up the butter until the mixture resembles coarse cornmeal. (I usually start with a couple of forks but finish by working the mixture with my fingers.)

Top the muffins with the remaining peaches and then add the streusel topping over the peaches.

Bake for 20 minutes or until done.

PEASANT BREAD

Note: Even though this is a yeast bread, it works up quickly and is a great recipe when you need something extra for dinner at the (almost!) last minute.

Mix the yeast, sugar, and salt. Add the water, mix well, and then add the oil. Begin adding the flour a little at a time, incorporating well after each addition. Knead the dough until smooth, about 5 to 7 minutes. Place dough into a greased bowl and cover. Let rise for 30 minutes.

Form into a round loaf and place on a greased cookie sheet. Cover and let rise again, about 45 minutes.

Preheat the oven to 425°. Brush top of loaf with oil and bake for 10 minutes. Reduce the heat to 375°, brush again with oil, and continue baking for 20 more minutes.

2¼ tsp. (1 packet) active dry yeast

1 T. sugar

2 tsp. salt

2 cups warm water (110°)

1 T. vegetable oil plus more for brushing top of loaf

4½ cups flour

POPOVERS

3 eggs

1 cup milk

3 T. melted butter

1 cup flour

½ tsp. salt

Preheat the oven to 375°. Grease eight 6-ounce custard cups and place them in a jelly roll pan.

In a large mixing bowl, beat eggs on low speed until frothy. Beat in the milk and melted butter. Gradually add the flour and salt to the egg mixture, beating until well combined and smooth.

Pour about ¾ cup of the batter into each custard cup. Bake 50 minutes and then remove the pan from the oven and cut a small slit in the top of each popover to let out steam. Return it to the oven and bake an additional 10 minutes. Immediately remove popovers from custard cups and serve.

They are good as is, but you can also serve them with pats of butter or gravy poured over them.

PUMPKIN MUFFINS

Preheat the oven to 350°. Spray 18 muffin cups with cooking spray, grease with shortening, or use paper cupcake liners. Set aside for now.

To make the topping:

In a small mixing bowl, mix all topping ingredients until well combined. Set aside for now.

To make the muffins:

In a medium bowl, whisk together the flour, salt, baking powder, baking soda, and pumpkin pie spice; set aside.

In a large mixing bowl (or the bowl of an electric mixer on low speed), beat together the butter and sugar until blended. Add the eggs one at a time and beat well after each addition. Continue beating for several minutes or until the mixture is smooth, light, and fluffy. Add the pumpkin puree and beat on low speed until mixed, scraping the bowl several times as necessary. Add the flour mixture and beat on low speed just until combined.

Scoop the batter into the prepared muffin cups, about two-thirds to three-fourths full. Divide the topping mixture evenly onto the tops of the muffins and bake for about 30 minutes or until the muffins are baked completely. Let the muffins cool in the pan for 10 minutes and then turn them out onto racks to cool completely.

For the topping:

5 T. flour

5 T. butter, melted

5 T. brown sugar

¾ cup chopped pecans or walnuts

¼ tsp. cinnamon

For the muffins:

2 cups flour

½ tsp. salt

½ tsp. baking powder

1 tsp. baking soda

1 T. pumpkin pie spice

¾ cup (1½ sticks) butter, room temperature

1½ cups sugar

2 eggs

1 (15 oz.) can pumpkin puree

SODA CRACKERS

Yeast mixture:

¼ cup warm water (110°)

1 T. yeast

Baking soda mixture:

1 tsp. baking soda

2 T. warm water (110°)

Cracker dough:

1¾ cups water

⅔ cup oil or melted shortening

4 cups flour

1 T. coarse salt or to taste

Preheat the oven to 350°.

Make the yeast mixture: In a small bowl, mix together the water and yeast and set aside.

Make the baking soda mixture: In another small bowl, mix together the baking soda and water and set aside.

Make the cracker dough: In a large bowl, mix together the water, the yeast mixture, the baking soda mixture, and the oil until well blended. Add enough flour so the dough pulls away from the sides of the bowl. Turn out the dough and knead for 10 minutes, adding flour as needed. (You'll use about 4 cups of flour total.)

Divide dough into several small portions so it's easier to work. Roll dough ⅛-inch thick. Cut into squares. Prick with fork and then sprinkle with the coarse salt.

Bake for about 10 minutes, or until the crackers are lightly browned.

Store in a jar with a tight-fitting lid.

SOFT SUGAR DOUGHNUTS

Pour milk into a large bowl; add yeast and stir to help dissolve. Add 1½ cups of the flour and beat until smooth, about 2 minutes. Cover and let rise until doubled, about 2 hours.

In another bowl, cream together the shortening, salt, and sugar. Add the egg and blend well. Stir into the yeast mixture. Add remaining flour, mixing as you go. Beat in a stand mixer for 5 minutes, or beat well by hand. Rub the top of the dough with shortening, cover bowl, and let rise again until doubled.

Roll out to ½-inch thickness and cut out doughnuts using a floured doughnut cutter. Transfer doughnuts to lightly floured trays and allow to rise, covered, for 45 minutes.

Fry doughnuts in hot oil or shortening that has been heated to about 375°, turning once, until done (about 3 to 5 minutes). Drain on paper towels. Let cool before sprinkling or dredging with sugar.

1 cup warm milk (110° to 115°)

2¼ tsp. (1 packet) active dry yeast

3½ cups sifted flour, divided (sifting helps make the doughnuts softer)

¼ cup shortening, plus extra for greasing the dough

1 tsp. salt

¼ cup sugar

1 egg

Oil for frying (you can also use shortening or lard for frying if you prefer)

Sugar for sprinkling

WHEAT BREAD

2¼ tsp. (1 packet) active dry yeast

2 cups warm water (110°)

2 T. sugar

2 tsp. salt

3 cups all-purpose flour

½ cup hot water

⅓ cup brown sugar

2 T. shortening

1 T. vegetable oil

3 cups whole wheat flour

In a large mixing bowl, mix yeast and warm water and allow to stand for 10 minutes. Add sugar, salt, and all-purpose flour. Using a wooden spoon or electric mixer, beat mixture until smooth. Set in a warm place until light and bubbly (this is called a "sponge").

Meanwhile, combine hot water with brown sugar, shortening, and oil. Allow mixture to sit until it's lukewarm. Add the mixture to the sponge and mix well with a wooden spoon. Add the whole wheat flour and mix. Turn out onto a floured surface and knead for about 8 minutes, adding enough flour so it doesn't stick. The dough should be smooth and elastic. Cover and let rise until doubled, about 1 hour. Divide in half equally, shape the dough into loaves, and place into 2 greased loaf pans; let rise until dough reaches just above the top of the pan. (Don't let it rise too high or it will fall during baking.)

Preheat the oven to 375°. Bake for 35 to 40 minutes or until done.

WHOLE WHEAT CRACKERS

Preheat the oven to 350°.

Mix together all ingredients. Add enough water to hold the dough together. Roll out on a floured surface (thinner dough makes crisper crackers) and cut into desired shapes.

Bake on an ungreased cookie sheet for 8 to 10 minutes.

2 cups whole wheat flour

1 tsp. salt

½ cup sesame seeds

¼ cup wheat germ

¼ cup vegetable oil

¼ cup grated Parmesan cheese

½ cup water (or slightly more if needed)

WHOLE WHEAT QUICK BUTTERMILK BREAD

This recipe couldn't be easier, and it uses minimal ingredients. Seriously one of the easiest recipes in this book!

Preheat the oven to 350°. Grease 2 loaf pans.

Mix all ingredients and pour batter into the prepared loaf pans.

Bake for 60 to 70 minutes or until done.

1 quart buttermilk

4 cups whole wheat flour

3 cups brown sugar

Pinch of salt

1 tsp. baking soda

BREAKFAST

Breakfast is such an easy meal to skip. And yet, it's often called the most important meal of the day, and rightly so. Eating breakfast accomplishes several functions—it wakes our brains and bodies up after our nighttime "fast" and replenishes our stores of glucose, which is necessary for giving us energy. Eating a good breakfast satisfies our hunger and helps us continue eating well throughout the day. Otherwise, when we skip this all-important meal, we can get suddenly famished and reach for the first thing we see—which may not be a healthy choice.

APPLE COFFEE CAKE

1 (20 oz.) can apple pie filling

2 eggs

1 cup vegetable oil

2 cups flour

1 tsp. baking soda

1 tsp. vanilla

2 cups sugar

1 tsp. cinnamon

1 tsp. salt

1 cup chopped walnuts or pecans

Preheat the oven to 350°. Grease a 9 × 13-inch baking dish.

Put all ingredients into a large mixing bowl and mix well with a wooden spoon. Pour batter into the prepared baking dish and bake for 1 hour.

APPLE FRITTERS

1 cup flour

1½ tsp. baking powder

½ tsp. salt

1 T. sugar

½ cup milk

1 T. vegetable oil, plus oil for frying

1 egg, well beaten

2 apples, peeled, cored, and diced

Powdered sugar for sprinkling (optional)

Cinnamon sugar for sprinkling (optional)

In a medium mixing bowl, mix the flour, baking powder, salt, and sugar.

In another bowl, blend the milk, oil, and egg. Gradually add this mixture to the dry ingredients, stirring after each addition. Stir in the apples and mix well.

Heat oil in a skillet and then drop the batter into the hot oil by large spoonfuls, being careful not to splatter. Fry until the bottom side is golden brown; turn the fritter over and fry the second side until golden brown as well.

Serve plain, or with powdered sugar or cinnamon sugar sprinkled on top.

APPLE PUFF PANCAKE CASSEROLE

Preheat the oven to 375°.

Melt the butter and pour into a 9 × 13-inch baking dish. Arrange the apples over the butter. Mix the brown sugar and 1 tsp. of the cinnamon and sprinkle over the apples. Bake for 10 minutes or until the apples have softened.

In a large mixing bowl, briskly whisk the eggs, milk, flour, granulated sugar, vanilla, salt, and remaining ½ teaspoon cinnamon until very well blended. Pour over the apples, return the baking dish to the oven, and bake for 40 minutes longer.

When ready to serve, sprinkle servings with powdered sugar if using and/or pour maple syrup on top.

4 T. butter

2 large apples, peeled, cored, and thinly sliced

3 T. brown sugar

1½ tsp. cinnamon, divided

6 eggs

1½ cups milk

1 cup flour

3 T. granulated sugar

1 tsp. vanilla

½ tsp. salt

Powdered sugar (optional)

Maple syrup (optional)

BACON, EGG, AND CHEESE CASSEROLE

½ lb. bacon

6 slices white or whole wheat bread

1 cup cheddar cheese, shredded or cubed

6 eggs

2 cups milk

½ tsp. salt

¼ tsp. pepper

Note: Assemble this casserole the night before and bake it in the morning.

Fry bacon until crisp and then crumble into pieces; set aside.

Cut bread into cubes and place in a well-buttered 2-quart casserole dish. Layer cheese on top of the bread cubes.

In a mixing bowl, beat eggs, milk, salt, and pepper. Pour over the bread and cheese. Sprinkle bacon pieces on top. Cover and refrigerate overnight.

In the morning, remove the casserole from the refrigerator, take off the cover, and let it sit for about 30 minutes while your oven preheats to 350°. Bake for 50 to 60 minutes or until puffed up and golden.

BACON AND SWISS CHEESE BREAKFAST STRATA

Butter an 11 × 17-inch baking dish; set aside.

Lightly grease a large skillet or use a well-conditioned cast-iron pan and heat on medium. Add the onion and bell peppers and sauté until the vegetables are almost done. Add the bacon and continue to cook, stirring occasionally, for 3 more minutes. Remove from heat and add the bread cubes.

Spread the mixture evenly in the prepared baking dish.

In a medium mixing bowl, whisk together the cheese, eggs, milk, mustard, and pepper; pour evenly over the bread mixture. If you are baking the strata immediately, preheat oven to 375°. Let it stand for 20 minutes before baking (see below). If you are making it the night before, cover the strata with plastic wrap and refrigerate overnight. In the morning, preheat oven to 375°, remove from the refrigerator, discard the plastic wrap, let stand 20 minutes, and then proceed with the bake.

Bake the strata for 35 to 40 minutes or until a knife inserted into the center of the casserole comes out clean. Let stand for 5 minutes before serving.

1 small onion, chopped

½ green bell pepper, chopped

½ red bell pepper, chopped (or you can use all green)

4 slices bacon, chopped

4 slices whole wheat or white bread, cut into ½-inch cubes

⅓ cup shredded Swiss cheese

4 eggs

1¾ cups milk

1 T. Dijon mustard

¼ tsp. black pepper

BAKED EGGS IN A MUFFIN CUP

For each serving:

Softened butter

1 T. shredded cheese (cheddar, jack, Parmesan, etc.)

2 T. precooked and diced meat (ham, bacon, sausage)

1 egg

Salt and pepper to taste

Note: You can make up to a dozen eggs at once if you have a 12-cup muffin tin. These are quick and easy to prepare, and the entire family's breakfast is done at one time.

Preheat the oven to 350°.

Grease muffin cups with the softened butter. Add the cheese and meat to the bottom and then crack the egg into the cup over the meat and cheese. Add salt and pepper to taste.

Using a baking pan with sides that are slightly larger than the muffin tin, layer the bottom of the pan with a folded kitchen towel or several layers of paper towels and then place the filled tin on the cushion. Carefully pour boiling water into the baking pan so the water level comes about halfway up the sides of the muffin cups. Immediately place the pan in the oven and bake for 14 to 25 minutes, depending on how hard you like your eggs.

Serve immediately, either along with, or on top of, a piece of toast, slices of fresh tomatoes, or a toasted English muffin.

BREAKFAST SAUSAGE AND SPINACH FRITTATA

Melt the butter in a heavy skillet or cast-iron frying pan that has a lid; tilt the pan so the melted butter covers the entire bottom of the pan. Add bread and stir to distribute evenly and completely cover the bottom of the pan. Sprinkle on the sausage, cheese, and spinach.

Whisk together the eggs and milk, season with salt and pepper, and pour over the sausage mixture. Cover the pan and cook on medium-low for about 15 minutes or until the eggs are set. If the bottom seems to be cooking too fast, turn down the heat to finish cooking.

2 T. butter

2 slices bread, torn up

½ lb. sausage, browned and drained

⅔ cup shredded cheddar cheese

½ cup chopped fresh spinach (or frozen spinach, thawed and squeezed dry)

4 eggs

½ cup milk

Salt and pepper to taste

BUCKWHEAT PANCAKES

Combine all ingredients and mix well. Drop the batter on a well-greased hot griddle and cook the pancakes until they are brown and starting to bubble at the edges; turn the pancakes over and cook the other side.

Serve with toppings of choice.

Note: Buckwheat has a nutty, robust flavor. If you prefer, you can use 1 cup buckwheat flour and 1 cup all-purpose flour for a slightly less distinct taste.

2 cups buckwheat flour

2 eggs, beaten

1 tsp. sugar

2 tsp. baking powder

⅛ tsp. salt

1½ cups milk

½ cup water

Toppings of choice: butter, syrup, honey, jam

CINNAMON SUGAR PANCAKE SQUARES

For pancake batter:

¾ cup milk

2 T. vegetable oil

1 egg

1 T. sugar

1 cup flour

2 tsp. baking powder

¼ tsp. salt

For cinnamon topping:

1 T. sugar

1 tsp. cinnamon

To make pancakes:

Preheat the oven to 350°. Grease or butter an 8 × 8-inch baking dish; set aside.

In a medium mixing bowl, beat together the milk, oil, and egg. Gradually mix in the sugar and flour, stirring well after each addition. Next, add the baking powder and salt and stir again until well blended. Pour the batter into the prepared baking dish.

To make topping:

In a small bowl, combine the sugar and cinnamon. You can sprinkle the topping over the batter and leave it at that, or you can take a butter knife and swirl the topping into the batter a bit. Cook's choice.

Bake for 25 minutes and serve.

COFFEE CAKE

To make coffee cake:

Preheat the oven to 375°. Grease an 8 × 8-inch baking dish.

In a medium mixing bowl, combine the egg, sugar, milk, and shortening. Mix well. Sift together the flour, salt, and baking powder. (I usually just whisk it together and call it good.) Add the flour mixture into the egg mixture and stir to blend well. Pour the batter into the prepared baking dish.

To make topping:

Combine the brown sugar, cinnamon, and flour; add the melted butter and mix until large crumbles form. Sprinkle the topping over the batter and then top with the walnut pieces, pressing them slightly into the topping.

Bake for 20 to 25 minutes or until done.

Coffee Cake:

1 egg, beaten

½ cup sugar

½ cup milk

2 T. melted shortening or butter

1 cup flour

½ tsp. salt

2 tsp. baking powder

Topping:

½ cup brown sugar

1 tsp. cinnamon

1 T. flour

1 T. butter, melted

½ cup walnut pieces

CORN FRITTERS

4 cups cornmeal

3 T. sugar

2½ tsp. salt

1 to 2 cups
boiling water

Vegetable oil
for frying

Combine cornmeal, sugar, and salt in a large mixing bowl. Gradually add enough boiling water, stirring with a wooden spoon, just until the mixture holds together.

Add oil to a saucepan to a depth of about ½ inch. Place paper towels on a plate to hold the cooked fritters. This will help to soak up extra oil.

Grease or butter your hands (the batter will be sticky!) and form the batter into patties about 1-inch thick and 4 inches around. Fry on each side until lightly browned and cooked through. Serve immediately.

Variations: Add diced cooked bacon, diced ham, onion, and/or shredded cheese.

CREAMED EGGS ON TOAST

In a medium saucepan, melt butter on medium-low heat. Gradually whisk in the flour so it doesn't become lumpy. Continue whisking the butter/flour mixture while adding the milk, and keep whisking until the mixture just comes to a boil and thickens.

Remove from heat and add the hard-boiled eggs and salt and pepper to taste. Spoon over toast.

Note: You can easily make a large batch of creamed eggs if you're feeding a lot of people by simply doubling this recipe, but if eggs are limited, you can get away with only 6 eggs for a double batch.

4 T. butter

4 T. flour

2 cups milk

4 to 6 hard-boiled eggs, peeled and chopped

Salt and pepper to taste

4 pieces toast

HUSH PUPPIES

1 cup cornmeal

1 tsp. baking powder

½ tsp. salt

1 egg

½ cup milk

Vegetable oil or shortening for frying

In a medium mixing bowl, combine the cornmeal, baking powder, and salt.

In another bowl, beat together the egg and milk; add to the bowl with the cornmeal mixture and stir until well blended. If the batter seems too stiff, you can add a bit more milk.

Heat oil or shortening in a heavy-bottomed skillet or saucepan; drop batter by large spoonfuls into the hot oil. Fry until the bottom side is golden brown and then turn over and fry the second side until golden brown as well.

Serve either plain or with syrup.

Variation: Mix in 4 slices of cooked, crumbled bacon pieces before frying.

MAPLE-FLAVORED PANCAKE SYRUP

In a medium saucepan, combine all ingredients and heat well, stirring to dissolve the sugar. *Do not boil!*

Store syrup in the refrigerator.

3½ cups brown sugar (1 lb.)

½ cup granulated sugar

1 cup water

⅔ cup corn syrup

2 tsp. maple extract or imitation maple flavoring

POACHED EGGS ON TOAST

This may be a simple recipe, but it's always a good choice. It was served for breakfast regularly when I was a child, and I've kept the tradition going.

Break the egg into a saucer or small bowl, keeping the yolk intact, and set aside for now.

Toast the bread and butter it liberally. Set it on a plate. (I usually work on the toast while the water is heating.)

Fill a shallow pan with water to an inch or two deep; bring to a brisk boil. Reduce heat to medium and quickly slip the egg into the water. Cook, covered, 3 to 5 minutes. Lift the egg out of the simmering water with a slotted spoon and hold over the pan to drain well. Set the poached egg on the buttered toast and serve.

Per serving:

1 egg

1 piece of bread

Butter

POTATO PANCAKES

2 cups plain hash-brown potatoes (or one 12-oz. pkg.)

2 eggs

2 T. minced onion

1 T. plus 1 tsp. flour

¼ tsp. salt

Vegetable oil for frying

In a medium mixing bowl, combine all ingredients except the oil and mix well.

Heat oil in a skillet over medium heat and then drop heaping tablespoonfuls of the mixture into the oil; flatten the pancakes with a spatula and cook for 5 minutes or until golden brown on the bottom. Turn the potato pancakes over and cook the other side until cooked through and golden brown.

SOUR CREAM OVERNIGHT PANCAKES

The night before:

In a pitcher, combine the sour cream, flour, honey or molasses, and baking soda. Cover with a towel or plastic wrap and leave on the counter overnight.

The next morning:

Add the salt and just enough egg to give the batter a thick pouring consistency. Stir well.

Grease or oil a skillet (make sure it's well-greased), heat, and then pour out enough batter to make pancakes about 4 inches in diameter. Fry on one side until it turns golden, and then turn the pancake over and fry the second side until golden. Don't forget to refresh the oil for every batch.

1 cup sour cream

2 cups flour

1 T. honey or molasses

1 tsp. baking soda

1 tsp. salt

1 to 2 eggs, beaten

SPINACH EGG BAKE

2 bunches green onions, finely chopped (or ¼ cup diced onion)

3 T. butter

½ lb. fresh spinach, stems trimmed

3 T. minced parsley

6 eggs

¼ cup sour cream

½ tsp. salt

¾ cup shredded cheddar cheese (about 3 oz.)

¼ cup grated Parmesan cheese

Preheat the oven to 350°.

In a large skillet, sauté the onion in butter for 2 minutes or until tender. Add the spinach and parsley; sauté 3 minutes longer or until heated through. Remove from the heat and set aside.

In a large bowl, beat the eggs, sour cream, and salt until smooth. Stir in the spinach mixture and cheddar cheese. Pour into a buttered or greased square baking dish. Sprinkle with Parmesan cheese.

Bake uncovered for 25 to 30 minutes or until a knife inserted near the center comes out clean. Cut into squares and serve.

ZUCCHINI FRITTATA

In a large ovenproof skillet, heat 2 tablespoons of the olive oil and the butter. When the butter is melted and the mixture is hot, add the garlic, zucchini, and onion. Sauté, stirring occasionally, for about 5 minutes. Remove from heat but keep the stove on.

In a large mixing bowl, beat the eggs and milk. Stir in the oregano, salt, pepper, and Parmesan cheese.

Preheat the oven's broiler.

Place the skillet back on the heat and drizzle the last tablespoon of oil over the vegetables. When the oil is hot, pour in the egg and cheese mixture and cook without stirring. When the eggs begin to set, lift the edges with a spatula and allow the uncooked egg to flow underneath. Continue lifting and cooking until the eggs are set and the top looks moist and creamy.

Place the skillet under the preheated broiler about 6 inches from the burner and broil for 2 to 3 minutes or until the top of the frittata looks completely cooked and has a golden color.

3 T. olive oil, divided

1 T. butter

2 cloves garlic, minced

2 cups sliced zucchini

½ cup diced onion

8 eggs

3 T. milk or half-and-half

½ tsp. oregano

½ tsp. salt

⅛ to ¼ tsp. pepper

3 T. grated Parmesan cheese

MAIN DISHES AND CASSEROLES

The recipes in this section are considered the main event. You'll find easy, comforting main dishes and casseroles, with an emphasis on hearty and delicious ingredients—straightforward food at its finest.

BAKED CHILE RELLENOS

2 (4 or 4.5 oz.) cans whole green chilies, drained

1½ cups shredded Monterey Jack cheese

½ cup shredded cheddar cheese

5 eggs

½ cup milk

1 T. flour

½ tsp. salt

¼ tsp. pepper

Several drops of hot sauce

Paprika for sprinkling

Note: If you don't have canned whole chilies, you can substitute with the same volume of chopped green chilies.

Preheat the oven to 375°. Lightly butter or grease an 8 × 8-inch square baking dish.

Cut the chilies in half lengthwise and remove seeds. Place half of the chilies in the bottom of the baking dish.

In a bowl, combine the cheeses. Place half of the cheese mixture on top of the layer of chilies in the baking dish. Repeat the layer with the remainder of the chilies and cheese.

In another bowl, beat the eggs. Add the milk, flour, salt, pepper, and hot sauce. Pour egg mixture over the chilies and cheese. Sprinkle paprika on top.

Bake uncovered for 25 to 30 minutes. Remove from the oven and allow to rest for 5 minutes before cutting and serving.

BAKED TUNA BISCUITS

Preheat the oven to 375°.

In a small mixing bowl, combine the tuna, mayonnaise, celery, carrot, and relish if using.

Separate the biscuits. On a lightly floured surface, use a rolling pin to roll each biscuit into a flat pancake shape. Spoon the tuna mixture evenly on 5 of the rolled-out biscuits and top each with the remaining 5 biscuits. Seal the edges by pressing with a fork.

Place the biscuits on an ungreased cookie sheet or jelly roll pan and bake for 15 minutes.

1 (7 oz.) can tuna, drained and flaked

⅓ cup mayonnaise

¼ cup diced celery

1 small carrot, peeled and grated or finely diced

2 T. sweet pickle relish (optional)

1 pkg. refrigerator biscuits (at least 10 biscuits)

Flour, for rolling

BEEF AND NOODLE CASSEROLE

1½ lbs. ground beef

1 tsp. salt

½ tsp. pepper

1 T. sugar

1 (15 oz.) can tomato sauce

1 cup sour cream

1 (8 oz.) pkg. cream cheese, softened

6 green onions, with part of green tops, chopped

1 (8 oz.) pkg. spinach noodles or regular noodles, cooked

½ cup shredded cheddar cheese

Preheat the oven to 350°. Butter or grease a baking dish.

Brown the ground beef; drain grease. Add the salt, pepper, sugar, and tomato sauce.

In a separate bowl, mix together the sour cream, cream cheese, and green onions.

Layer noodles, then cheese mixture, then meat mixture; repeat one more time. Sprinkle the cheddar cheese over the top and bake, uncovered, for 25 to 30 minutes.

BUFFET BEEF CUBES

Place the beef cubes in a large ziplock bag or bowl, add the flour, and shake or stir the meat to coat.

In a large saucepan with a lid, melt the shortening and add the beef cubes and brown the meat on all sides.

While the meat is browning, in a large mixing bowl, stir the remaining ingredients together until well blended. Pour the mixture into the saucepan containing the meat; cover with the lid and simmer on a fairly low heat for 2 hours, stirring often to prevent sticking, or until the meat is tender and the sauce has thickened to a gravy-like consistency.

Serve over cooked noodles or rice.

1½ lbs. beef chuck, cubed

2 T. flour

2 T. shortening

2¼ cups V8 juice

¼ cup water

1 T. sugar

1½ tsp. salt

½ tsp. basil

¼ tsp. pepper

1 T. Worcestershire sauce

1 tsp. vinegar

1½ cups chopped onion

1 bay leaf

CAST-IRON BAKED PORK CHOPS

4 bone-in pork
chops, about
1 to 1½-inch thick

Salt

Water

Spices of choice

3 T. vegetable oil

Brine pork chops: Put the pork chops in a large ziplock bag or bowl. Add just enough water to cover, measuring out one cup at a time. Next, add 1 tablespoon salt for every cup of water used. (I don't usually need more than one cup of water.) Swish the water (or shake the bag) until the salt and water are well mixed. Allow the pork chops to sit in the brine for 1 to 4 hours.

Preheat the oven to 375°.

Remove the chops from the brine and pat dry. Season with spices of your choice, such as pepper, garlic powder, onion powder, and smoked paprika.

Thoroughly preheat a cast-iron skillet over high heat. (Be careful to raise the temperature in increments to avoid cracking the skillet.) When the skillet is hot, add the oil and immediately add the pork chops. Fry the chops for about 3 minutes, until browned; turn the chops over and place the skillet in the oven. Bake for 3 minutes and then turn the chops over and bake for 3 to 5 minutes more. Remove the chops to a plate or baking pan and tent loosely with aluminum foil for 5 minutes to rest.

Add about 2 tablespoons of water to the skillet and stir to loosen drippings. Plate the chops and drizzle the pan juices over the meat.

CHICKEN SALAD WITH CURRIED YOGURT DRESSING

To make dressing:

Combine all dressing ingredients and mix until well blended. Chill until ready to use.

To make salad:

In a large bowl, layer the salad ingredients in the order given. Spoon dressing over the layers and toss when ready to serve.

Note: Depending on how much dressing you prefer, taste before adding the entire amount and then adjust according to your taste.

Dressing:

1 (8 oz.) container plain yogurt

2 T. honey

¾ tsp. curry powder

½ tsp. lemon and herb seasoning

Salad:

4 to 5 cups mixed lettuce

2 cups cooked chicken, diced and cooled

1 (11 oz.) can mandarin oranges, drained

1 avocado, peeled and sliced or chopped

4 T. almond slices

CREAMED TUNA ON TOAST

1 cup Master White
Sauce and Gravy Mix
(page 88)

2 cups water

1 (7 oz.) can tuna

Salt and pepper to
taste

6 pieces of bread,
toasted

In a medium saucepan, whisk together the white sauce mix and water. Turn the heat to medium and heat, stirring constantly, until the mixture comes to a boil and the sauce thickens. Remove the saucepan from the heat and turn the stove to low. Add the tuna to the sauce mixture and move the saucepan back onto the heat and stir, breaking up the tuna, until heated through. Salt and pepper to taste.

Place the toast onto individual plates and scoop the sauce over the pieces. Serve immediately.

CURRIED SPAGHETTI

Cook pasta until al dente, following directions on package.

Grease a 9 × 13-inch casserole dish with oil.

Preheat the oven to 350°.

In a large skillet, brown ground beef and onion. Drain most of the grease and then add the stewed tomatoes, mustard, curry powder, sugar, ketchup, and salt and pepper to taste. Cook, stirring occasionally, until the mixture is thoroughly heated.

Layer pasta, tomato mixture, and then cheese. Repeat layers, ending with cheese.

Bake for 30 minutes and serve.

1 (8 oz.) pkg. pasta

1 lb. ground beef

1 onion, chopped

1 (28 oz.) can stewed tomatoes

1 tsp. prepared mustard

2 tsp. curry powder

1 tsp. sugar

⅓ cup ketchup

Salt and pepper to taste

2 cups shredded sharp cheddar cheese

DR. MARTIN'S MIX

1½ lbs. ground pork

1 green bell pepper, chopped

2 green onions, chopped, including some of the green part

2 celery ribs, chopped

2 cups chicken broth

1 cup uncooked rice

1 T. Worcestershire sauce

½ tsp. salt

In a large saucepan or pot with a lid, brown the pork; drain off most of the grease, leaving some in the pot. Add the remaining ingredients and stir to mix. Simmer on low heat for 1 hour or until the rice is cooked through and tender.

HOBO DINNER

This is a fun meal on a family fun night. Everybody makes their own dinner!

Preheat the oven to 350°.

Have a large double layer of aluminum foil for each person. Everyone adds the foods of their choice to the aluminum foil before closing it up and baking it in the oven. (If you make this in the summer, you can set them on the grill to cook instead.)

Use any foods you like; be sure to cut food into similar-sized chunks or slices so everything cooks evenly in the foil packets. Here are some suggestions: lean ground beef patty (see note below), smoked sausage links, kielbasa, cooked ham, leftover beef or pork roasts, cooked chicken, red potatoes, onion, carrots, celery, bell peppers, mushrooms, parsnips, etc. Add a pat of butter, a splash of broth or water, ketchup, or barbeque sauce. Shake some salt, pepper, and garlic powder over the top if desired.

Close up the foil packets, place them in the oven (you can put them directly on the oven rack), and bake them for 45 minutes to 1 hour or until the meat is cooked through and the vegetables are tender.

Note: If you want to include a ground beef patty inside each packet, make the patties on the thin side and place those on the aluminum foil first before topping with the vegetables.

Meat of choice

Vegetables of choice

Butter

Broth or sauce of choice

Salt and pepper to taste

Additional spices of choice

MACARONI AND CHEESE

½ cup (1 stick) room temperature butter, divided

½ cup panko breadcrumbs

4 cups uncooked elbow macaroni

¼ cup flour

3 cups milk

1½ tsp. dry ground mustard

4 cups shredded cheddar cheese

1½ tsp. salt

¼ tsp. pepper

Melt 2 tablespoons of the butter, and in a small bowl and using a fork, mix the melted butter with the panko crumbs, mixing until completely incorporated; set aside for now.

Cook macaroni according to package directions—don't overcook! Drain noodles.

Using 2 tablespoons of the butter, grease the bottom and sides of a large baking dish and set aside for now.

At this point, preheat your oven to 350°.

In a large pot, melt the remaining 4 tablespoons (½ stick) butter over medium-low heat and then sprinkle in the flour, whisking as you do so. Turn the heat to about medium and cook the roux, whisking for 1 minute. Pour in milk, whisking while you pour, then add the mustard and continue to whisk until the roux comes to a boil and thickens slightly. Reduce the heat to your lowest setting, add the cheese, and stir to melt the cheese. Add the salt and pepper and mix to combine. Pour in the cooked and drained macaroni and mix carefully but thoroughly. Spoon the macaroni and cheese into the prepared baking dish and top with the buttered panko crumbs.

Bake for 20 minutes or until the macaroni and cheese is bubbling and the panko crumbs have turned golden.

ONION PIE

Preheat the oven to 350°. Fit your pie crust into your pan.

Gently fry the onions in the butter until they are almost soft; spread the onions evenly over the pie crust.

Combine the eggs, milk, and salt and pepper and pour the mixture over the onions.

Bake for 40 to 50 minutes or until done.

1 deep-dish pie crust, uncooked

2 cups sliced onion

3 T. butter

6 eggs, beaten

1 cup milk

Salt and pepper

OVEN-BAKED SPARERIBS

In a small mixing bowl, whisk together all ingredients except the ribs and let the sauce stand, covered, on the counter or in the refrigerator overnight. (You could also prep this early in the morning to have ready for dinner.)

Preheat the oven to 375°.

Place unbasted ribs in a large roaster and bake, uncovered, until just done (approximately 1½ hours). Pour off all but ¼ cup of the drippings, then baste the ribs with the sauce. Continue to bake, basting the ribs frequently, until the ribs are done and the sauce becomes sticky.

½ cup soy sauce

½ cup cider vinegar

½ cup sugar

1 clove garlic, minced

1 small pinch ginger

1 small pinch ground cloves

6 lbs. meaty spareribs, cut into individual ribs

RANCH BAKED BEANS

¼ cup vegetable oil

2 cups chopped onion

1 lb. lean ground beef

1 tsp. salt

1 cup ketchup

2 T. prepared mustard

2 tsp. cider vinegar

2 (15 oz.) cans pork and beans

2 (15.5 oz.) cans kidney beans, rinsed and drained

¼ cup brown sugar

Preheat the oven to 400°.

Heat the oil in a large pot, then add the onion and cook until softened. Add the ground beef and continue cooking until the beef has browned; drain the grease. Add the remaining ingredients, mix well, and then pour the mixture into a large casserole dish and bake for 30 minutes or until heated through and bubbling.

SALMAGUNDI

I have no idea how the name for this recipe came to be, because salmagundi generally refers to an elaborate salad dish that includes meat and anchovies and originated in England in the Elizabethan era. But this recipe has been in my family for several generations and has always been called Salmagundi, so Salmagundi it is!

Preheat the oven to 375°. Butter or grease a 2-quart casserole dish with a lid.

In a mixing bowl, combine one can of the tomato sauce with the rice, water, onion, bell pepper, salt, and pepper. Turn mixture into the prepared casserole dish. Layer the ground beef over the top, spreading evenly. Next, layer the corn evenly over the beef.

In a small mixing bowl, mix the remaining can of tomato sauce with the chili powder; pour over the corn.

Cover and bake for 1 hour; uncover and bake 10 minutes longer or until the rice is tender.

2 (8 oz.) cans tomato sauce, divided

¾ cup uncooked rice

1 cup water

1 cup chopped onion

½ cup diced green bell pepper

1 tsp. salt

½ tsp. pepper

1 lb. lean ground beef

1 (15 oz.) can corn, drained (or 2 cups frozen corn)

½ tsp. chili powder

SAUSAGE AND WHITE BEAN CASSOULET

1 T. olive oil

½ lb. sweet Italian sausage links

1 lb. kielbasa sausage, cut into ½-inch rounds

3 leeks, white and pale green parts only, sliced

3 cloves garlic, minced

1 apple, peeled, cored, and chopped

1 T. fresh rosemary (or ½ tsp. dried)

1 tsp. dried sage

1 bay leaf

1 (14.5 oz.) can diced tomatoes, undrained

2 to 3 drops Tabasco sauce

2 (15 oz.) cans great northern beans, rinsed and drained

1 (10 oz.) pkg. frozen baby lima beans, rinsed

1½ cups chicken broth

2 T. tomato paste

Pepper

¼ cup chopped fresh parsley (or 2 T. dried)

This is another recipe my mom made for us. It was quite different from our usual fare, but we loved it. It's perfect on a cold winter day and served with sourdough bread for scooping up every last bit of broth.

Preheat the oven to 350°.

In a heavy-bottomed pot or Dutch oven with a lid (cast iron or enamel-coated cast iron works best) over medium heat, add the oil and let it warm up. Add the whole Italian sausages and cook for 10 to 15 minutes, turning occasionally so all sides brown. Add the kielbasa and continue browning both sausages for about 10 minutes longer. Remove the Italian sausages, cut into ½-inch rounds, and return them to the pot.

Add leeks and garlic to the same pot and sauté until soft, about 5 minutes. Add the apple, rosemary, sage, and bay leaf. Stir in the diced tomatoes, Tabasco sauce, beans, broth, and tomato paste. Season with a bit of pepper.

Bake, covered, for an hour; remove lid, add the parsley, and bake uncovered for 15 minutes longer. Remove bay leaf, adjust seasonings, and serve.

SLOW-COOKER HONEY GARLIC CHICKEN

Put the chicken in the bottom of the slow cooker.

In a small mixing bowl, combine the honey, garlic, soy sauce, ketchup, and red pepper flakes; pour the mixture over the chicken.

Slow cook the chicken on low until the chicken is thoroughly cooked and tender, about 4 to 5 hours.

When the chicken is done, remove the chicken and set aside. Mix the cornstarch and water and pour the mixture into the slow cooker, stirring as you pour. Turn the heat to high and cook another 30 minutes or until the sauce has thickened. Put the chicken pieces back into the slow cooker for a bit so the chicken gets hot once again, about 20 minutes.

Serve over rice.

6 to 8 bone-in chicken thighs with the skin off

1 cup honey

6 to 7 cloves garlic, minced

⅔ cup soy sauce

3 T. ketchup

½ tsp. red pepper flakes

2 T. cornstarch

½ cup water

Cooked rice for serving

TOFU ENCHILADAS

1 T. vegetable oil, plus more for frying tortillas

1 small onion, diced

3 cloves garlic, minced

1 tsp. salt

¾ tsp. cumin

¼ cup soy sauce

1 (14 oz.) block firm tofu, diced

1 (7 oz.) can green chili salsa

1 (15 oz.) can tomato sauce

10 to 12 corn tortillas, depending on size

¾ cup shredded cheddar cheese or to taste

Don't let the tofu scare you. These enchiladas are super tasty. And if you don't let your family know ahead of time what they're eating, they'll no doubt love them!

Preheat the oven to 375°. Lightly grease a baking dish that's big enough to accommodate the size of the rolled tortillas.

In a large saucepan, heat oil; add the onion and garlic and sauté until softened. Add the salt, cumin, and soy sauce and mix to blend. Add the tofu and heat for several minutes but don't overcook. Remove from the heat.

In a medium saucepan, mix the green chili salsa and the tomato sauce. Heat thoroughly and turn off heat, but no need to remove from the burner.

Fry tortillas in oil, but don't make them hard. They need to be limp in order to roll. Fill the tortillas with the tofu mixture, roll them up, and lay them seam side down in single layer in the prepared baking dish. Pour the tomato sauce mixture over the enchiladas, top with cheese, and bake in the oven until the cheese is melted and the enchiladas are hot.

TUNA CASSEROLE

Preheat the oven to 425°. Butter a 2-quart casserole dish.

Mix all ingredients together except for the Parmesan cheese, garlic powder if using, and slivered almonds. Add to the casserole dish. Evenly spread Parmesan cheese, garlic powder, and slivered almonds over the top.

Bake uncovered for 20 minutes and serve.

3 cups hot cooked pasta

1 (6.5 oz.) can tuna, drained

½ cup mayonnaise

1 cup chopped celery

⅓ cup chopped onion

¼ cup chopped bell pepper

½ tsp. salt

1 (10.5 oz.) can cream of celery soup blended with ½ cup milk

1 cup shredded cheddar cheese

⅛ to ¼ cup Parmesan cheese (to taste)

½ tsp. garlic powder (optional)

¼ cup slivered almonds

TUNA SWISS PIE

Preheat the oven to 375°.

Pierce the pie shell with a fork and bake for 10 minutes. Do not turn off oven when done.

While the crust is baking, mix the tuna, Swiss cheese, green onion, and mushrooms. When the crust is removed from the oven, pour the tuna mixture into the pie shell.

In another bowl, add the eggs and beat them until well mixed. Add the mayonnaise and milk and blend well; pour over the tuna mixture and place the pie on an aluminum foil-lined cookie sheet. Bake for 50 minutes or until a knife comes out clean and the pie is puffed and golden.

1 (9-inch) unbaked pie shell

2 (6.5 oz.) cans tuna, drained

1 cup shredded Swiss cheese

½ cup chopped green onion

½ cup sliced mushrooms

3 eggs

1 cup mayonnaise

½ cup milk

SOUPS AND STEWS

I make soups and stews regularly during the winter months. They are the perfect meal for cold, blustery days and make tasty use of pantry items. Serve them with fresh-from-the-oven bread or crackers and you have a full meal that mostly cooks itself.

APPLE CIDER PORK STEW WITH CHEESE DUMPLINGS

Stew:

3 T. flour

1 tsp. salt

¾ tsp. thyme

⅛ tsp. pepper

¾ lb. boneless pork loin (roast or chops), cubed

2 T. vegetable oil

2 cups apple cider or apple juice

1 cup water

3 sweet potatoes, peeled and cubed (about 3 cups)

2 large apples, peeled, seeded, and cubed (about 2 cups)

1 cup chopped onion

2 T. water

Cheese Dumplings:

1 cup flour

1½ tsp. baking powder

¼ tsp. salt

⅔ cup buttermilk

¼ cup cheddar cheese

½ tsp. parsley flakes (optional)

Note: One time I didn't have any sweet potatoes, so I used regular potatoes, and it was just as good!

To make stew:

In a medium mixing bowl or gallon-sized ziplock bag, mix together the flour, salt, thyme, and pepper. Add the pork and stir or shake to coat pork evenly. Place coated pork on waxed paper and reserve remaining flour mixture to be used later in this recipe.

In a Dutch oven or large saucepan, heat oil over medium-high heat; add pork and cook, stirring occasionally so all sides have a chance to brown, for about 5 minutes. Add all remaining stew ingredients except for the reserved flour and 2 tablespoons of water. Bring to a boil; reduce heat, cover, and simmer 45 to 60 minutes or until pork is tender, stirring occasionally.

In a small bowl, mix together the reserved flour mixture and 2 tablespoons water and blend until smooth. Add to the stew; stir and cook for several minutes until stew is slightly thickened.

To make cheese dumplings:

Mix the flour, baking powder, and salt. Add the buttermilk, cheese, and parsley (if using) and stir just until moistened—don't overmix. Drop by tablespoonfuls into the hot stew. Cover the Dutch oven tightly and cook 25 to 35 minutes or until dumplings are fluffy and no longer doughy. Don't peek sooner than 25 minutes.

BARLEY AND LENTIL SOUP

In a large pot, heat oil. Add the onion, carrots, and celery and sauté, stirring, until the vegetables are soft, about 5 to 7 minutes. Add the garlic and cook, stirring for another 1 to 2 minutes. Next, add the barley, about 6 cups of the broth, cumin, parsley, and bay leaf. Reduce the heat to a low simmer, cover the pot, and simmer for 20 minutes. Add the lentils and simmer for another 40 minutes or until the lentils and barley are soft, adding more broth as necessary.

Right before serving, stir in the lemon juice and add salt and pepper to taste.

2 T. vegetable oil

1 onion, diced

1 cup diced carrots

½ cup diced celery

½ tsp. minced garlic

1 cup pearl barley

6 to 8 cups broth (beef, chicken, or vegetable), divided

1½ tsp. ground cumin

2 tsp. dried parsley

1 bay leaf

1 cup lentils

2 T. lemon juice

Salt and pepper to taste

BARLEY AND VEGETABLE SOUP

¾ cup pearl barley

11 cups chicken broth, divided

3 T. butter

1½ cups diced onion

1 cup diced carrots

1 cup thinly sliced mushrooms

½ cup diced celery

Salt and pepper to taste

In a medium saucepan, add the pearl barley and 3 cups of the chicken broth; bring to a boil over medium heat and simmer the mixture for 1 hour or until the liquid is absorbed.

While the barley is cooking, in a large soup pot, melt the butter and then add the onion, carrots, mushrooms, and celery. Cover the pot with the lid and keep the heat low, stirring occasionally, until the vegetables are softened but not browned, about 5 to 10 minutes. Add the remaining 8 cups of chicken broth and simmer the mixture (you may need to turn up the heat a bit) and simmer for 30 minutes. Add the cooked barley and simmer for another 5 minutes or so. Salt and pepper to taste before serving.

BEAN WITH BACON SOUP

In the large pot that you will cook the soup in, fry the bacon until just crisp; remove the bacon but leave the bacon grease. Add the carrots, celery, and onion and cook on medium-low heat, stirring regularly, for about 5 minutes or until the vegetables are somewhat soft. Add the beans, broth, water, and bay leaves and cook on low heat, with the lid partially on and stirring occasionally, for 30 minutes to an hour. Chop the bacon into very small pieces and add them to the soup along with the tomato paste; cover and simmer for another 20 minutes.

Just before serving, you can use an immersion blender to partially puree the soup to give it a creamy texture while leaving some of the beans whole or in pieces, or use a potato masher to accomplish the same thing. Season with salt and pepper to taste and serve.

4 slices bacon

2 carrots, peeled and diced

1 celery rib, diced

1 onion, diced

3 (15.5 oz.) cans small white beans (such as navy or cannellini), rinsed and drained

1 quart (4 cups) chicken broth

2 cups water

2 bay leaves

2 T. tomato paste

Salt and pepper to taste

BEEF AND TURNIP STEW

¾ lb. beef (bottom round, eye round, or chuck steak), cubed

2 tsp. vegetable oil

1 tsp. dried rosemary (or 2 tsp. fresh)

1 large onion, sliced

3 cloves garlic, minced

2½ cups beef broth

1 T. tomato paste

¼ tsp. pepper

6 turnips, cleaned and cut into ½-inch cubes

4 carrots, peeled and sliced

In a large saucepot or Dutch oven, brown beef in oil. When meat has browned on all sides, add the rosemary, onion, and garlic and cook for 2 to 3 minutes, stirring constantly. Stir in broth, tomato paste, and pepper. Cover and cook for 45 minutes or until meat is thoroughly cooked and tender.

Add the turnips and carrots and cook about 20 minutes more, stirring occasionally, until the vegetables are tender.

BEEF STEW WITH COFFEE

Place the flour, salt, pepper, and thyme in a medium-sized mixing bowl or gallon-sized ziplock bag; stir or shake to blend ingredients. Add the beef in batches, and shake or stir to coat the cubes of meat. You can set them on a cookie sheet as you continue coating all the beef.

In a large Dutch oven or saucepot, heat the oil and add the coated beef, again working in batches if needed. Brown on all sides. (You may need to add more oil if you do this in batches.) Next, add all remaining ingredients and simmer, covered, for 1½ to 2 hours.

1 cup flour

1½ tsp. salt

½ tsp. pepper

1 tsp. thyme

3 lbs. stew beef, cubed

3 T. vegetable oil

5 cups beef broth

1 cup strong brewed coffee

1 T. Worcestershire sauce

1 tsp. paprika

1 tsp. sugar

3 T. ketchup

6 potatoes, peeled and quartered

1 large onion, quartered

6 carrots, peeled, trimmed, and quartered

BROCCOLI CHOWDER

2 lbs. fresh broccoli, broken into florets

2 (14.5 oz.) cans chicken broth (or 1 quart)

1 cup chopped cooked ham

2 tsp. salt

½ tsp. pepper

1 cup half-and-half (or milk, but it won't be quite as creamy)

3 cups milk

½ lb. Swiss cheese, shredded

¼ cup butter

In a large pot, cook the broccoli, covered, in the broth for 7 minutes. With a slotted spoon, remove the cooked broccoli, leaving the broth in the pot. When cool enough to handle, coarsely chop the broccoli and set aside for now.

Add the ham, salt, and pepper to the soup pot with the broth, and bring the mixture to a simmer over medium heat, stirring occasionally. When it comes to a gentle boil, turn down the heat and add the remaining ingredients including the broccoli; continue to cook on a low simmer just until the soup is heated through and the butter and cheese are melted.

BUTTERNUT SQUASH AND CORN CHOWDER

In a large pot, cook the bacon until crisp. Remove the bacon and set on paper towels, reserving 2 tablespoons of the drippings in the pot. Over medium heat, add the onion and celery and sauté until tender, about 4 minutes. Stir in the flour until blended, and then gradually add the broth, stirring constantly. Bring the mixture to a low boil, still stirring constantly, and cook until it's slightly thickened, about 2 to 3 minutes. Stir in the squash and cream-style corn and let it heat for a few minutes; add the half-and-half, parsley, salt, and pepper and continue to heat thoroughly but not boil.

Serve in individual bowls with a dollop of sour cream on top if using.

10 slices bacon

1 onion, chopped

1 celery rib, chopped

2 T. flour

2 cups chicken broth

6 cups cooked and mashed butternut squash

1 (14.75 oz.) can cream-style corn

2 cups half-and-half

1 T. fresh parsley, minced (or 1 tsp. dried)

1½ tsp. salt

½ tsp. pepper

Sour cream (optional)

CHICKEN CHILI

2 T. vegetable oil

1 onion, chopped

3 bell peppers, any color, chopped

3 cloves garlic, minced

1 lb. ground chicken

1 T. flour

1 T. unsweetened cocoa powder

1 T. cumin

2 T. chili powder

2 tsp. ground coriander

½ tsp. salt

½ tsp. pepper

2 (14.5 oz.) cans diced tomatoes, undrained

¼ cup lime juice

1 (14.5 oz.) can white kidney or cannellini beans, rinsed and drained

Tortilla chips for serving

Sour cream for serving (optional)

In a large pot, heat the oil over medium heat, and then add the onion and peppers and sauté until crisp tender, about 7 minutes. Add the garlic and cook, stirring, for another minute. Next, add the chicken and cook, stirring to break up meat, for 8 to 10 minutes or until no longer pink.

Stir in the flour, cocoa powder, and seasonings and then add the tomatoes and lime juice. Bring to a boil and then reduce the heat and cook, uncovered and stirring frequently, until thickened, about 20 minutes. Add the beans and continue to cook until thoroughly heated.

Ladle into individual bowls and top with broken-up tortilla chips and sour cream if using.

EASY CLAM CHOWDER

Drain clams, reserving the clam juice, and set aside.

In a large soup pot, add the potatoes, onion, carrots, butter, water, and reserved clam juice; cook over medium heat until the vegetables are tender, about 15 minutes. Stir in the evaporated milk, cream of mushroom soup, salt, and pepper and simmer, uncovered, until thoroughly heated.

Ladle into individual bowls and top with bacon bits if using.

1 (6.5 oz.) can minced clams

4 potatoes, peeled and diced

¼ cup diced onion

3 carrots, peeled and diced

4 T. (½ stick) butter, cut into cubes for quicker melting

¾ cup water

1 (12 oz.) can evaporated milk

1 (10.5 oz.) can condensed cream of mushroom soup

½ tsp. salt or to taste

¼ tsp. pepper or to taste

4 slices crisp cooked bacon, diced (optional)

LENTIL SOUP

2 cups dry lentils

2½ quarts water or broth

1½ tsp. salt (omit if using broth)

½ tsp. pepper

1 bay leaf

2 whole cloves

Dash of cayenne pepper

1 ham bone

¼ cup butter

1 large carrot, peeled and chopped

1 large onion, chopped

¾ cup chopped celery

1 clove garlic, minced

Chopped fresh parsley for serving

Wash the lentils and place them in a large pot along with the water or broth. Add the salt and pepper, bay leaf, cloves, cayenne pepper, and ham bone. Turn the heat to medium and begin the cooking process.

While the soup is heating, in another pot, melt the butter and sauté the carrot, onion, celery, and garlic for 10 minutes. Add the vegetables to the soup, cover the pot, and simmer for 2 hours. Check and stir the soup occasionally and add more broth or water to the soup pot if the level of the liquid gets too low. Ladle the soup into individual bowls and top each with a bit of parsley.

MINESTRINA DI CUBETTI

Preheat the oven to 300°. Butter an 8 × 8-inch square glass baking dish and set aside.

In a medium mixing bowl, beat or whisk the ricotta for 2 to 3 minutes until the ricotta is smooth. Add the egg, egg yolk, salt, nutmeg, and Parmesan cheese and blend the mixture well using a rubber spatula so you can scrape down the sides as needed. Spread the ricotta mixture evenly into the baking dish. Place the baking dish, uncovered, inside a large pan filled with 1 inch of very hot water. Bake until firm, about 45 minutes.

Cool the ricotta to room temperature, and then cut into bite-size cubes.

When ready to serve, heat the chicken broth to boiling; remove from the heat and immediately add the ricotta cubes. Serve in individual bowls with parsley sprinkled on top and a small bowl of shredded Parmesan cheese on the side.

½ lb. (8 oz.) ricotta cheese, room temperature

1 whole egg

1 egg yolk

1 tsp. salt

Pinch of nutmeg

¾ cup shredded Parmesan cheese, plus more for serving

2 to 2½ quarts chicken broth

Minced parsley (fresh or dried) for serving

MUSHROOM SOUP WITH PARMESAN CHEESE

1 T. butter

1 T. olive oil

1 onion, diced

1 clove garlic, halved

1 lb. mushrooms, thinly sliced

3 T. tomato paste

3 cups chicken broth

2 T. sweet vermouth

Salt and pepper to taste

4 egg yolks

2 T. minced parsley

2½ T. grated Parmesan cheese

4 thick slices sourdough or French bread

Butter for toast

Note: If you don't have vermouth for this recipe, you can substitute red wine or more broth with a splash of Worcestershire sauce.

In a heavy-bottomed pot, melt the butter and olive oil. Sauté the onion and garlic over medium heat until the onion has caramelized slightly; discard garlic. Stir in the mushrooms and sauté for 5 to 10 minutes or until the mushrooms have softened. Add the tomato paste and stir to mix, then add the broth. Stir again and add the vermouth; add salt and pepper to taste. Let the soup simmer for 10 minutes.

In a small mixing bowl, use a whisk or eggbeaters to beat together the egg yolks, parsley, and Parmesan cheese. Set aside for now while you toast the bread.

Butter one side of each piece of bread and broil the toast until the top has crisped up and browned; no need to toast both sides. Alternatively, you can use a toaster to toast the bread and butter one side when done.

Now take the egg yolk mixture and beat it into the boiling soup, stirring all the while. Place a piece of toast into each bowl and pour the soup over the bread. Serve at once.

PAT'S VEGETARIAN MINESTRONE SOUP

For more than ten years now, some girlfriends and I meet up once a month for lunch, prayer, and friendship. Our hostess is Pat, and she regularly makes this delicious and nutritious minestrone soup. Served alongside fresh-baked French bread, it's always a special treat!

In a large pot, combine broth, tomatoes, kidney beans, onion, celery, carrots, green beans, zucchini, garlic, parsley, oregano, salt, thyme, and black pepper. Bring to a low boil and then reduce the heat to low, cover the pot, and simmer for 1 hour or until all vegetables are cooked through.

In a medium saucepan, bring about 2 cups of lightly salted water to a boil. Cook the elbow macaroni in the boiling water, stirring occasionally, until done according to package directions; remove from heat and drain.

Stir the cooked macaroni and spinach into the soup pot and cook another 10 to 15 minutes. Dish up soup into individual bowls and let each person top with Parmesan cheese.

6 cups vegetable broth

1 (28 oz.) can crushed tomatoes

1 (15 oz.) can kidney beans, drained

1 onion, chopped

2 celery ribs, diced

2 large carrots, diced

1 cup fresh or frozen green beans (or 8 oz. canned green beans)

1 small zucchini, sliced in rounds

3 cloves garlic, minced

1 T. minced fresh parsley (or 1 tsp. dried)

1½ tsp. oregano

1 tsp. salt

¾ tsp. thyme

¼ tsp. black pepper

½ cup elbow macaroni

4 cups chopped fresh spinach or Swiss chard leaves

¼ cup finely grated Parmesan cheese or to taste

PUMPKIN CURRY SOUP

1 T. vegetable oil

½ onion, diced

2 cloves garlic, minced

1 (15 oz.) can pumpkin puree

1 quart (4 cups) vegetable broth

1½ tsp. curry powder

½ tsp. turmeric

1 (13.5 oz.) can unsweetened coconut milk

1 tsp. maple syrup

Salt and pepper to taste

Sour cream for serving

Roasted pumpkin seeds or sunflower seeds for serving

Chopped cilantro for serving (optional)

In a large saucepan, heat the oil; add the onion and cook, stirring gently, until the onion is translucent, about 5 minutes; stir in garlic and cook for 1 minute more.

Stir in the pumpkin puree, broth, curry powder, and turmeric; turn the heat up and bring soup to a low boil. Simmer the soup for 10 minutes, turning down the heat if needed. Stir in the coconut milk and maple syrup and gently simmer for another 5 to 10 minutes.

Add salt and pepper to taste and serve in individual bowls, topped with sour cream, pumpkin seeds, and cilantro if using.

QUICK AND EASY TACO STEW

In a stewpot, brown ground beef; drain off fat. Add remaining ingredients except chips and cheese and simmer for 30 minutes or longer, making sure that the meat is thoroughly cooked before serving.

Ladle into individual bowls and top with tortilla chips and cheese if desired.

1 lb. ground beef

1 medium onion, peeled and chunked

1 (15.25 oz.) can corn, drained (or 2 cups fresh or frozen corn)

1 (14.5 oz.) can diced tomatoes with green chilies, undrained (such as Ro*Tel)

1 (15 to 16 oz.) can pinto beans with chili sauce, undrained

1 (10.75 oz.) can condensed tomato soup, undiluted

1 cup water

Tortilla chips and cheese (optional)

SUNFLOWER SOUP

In a large pot, mix together all ingredients except scallions; bring to a boil. Cover the pot, turn down the heat to maintain a gentle simmer, and cook for 45 minutes. When ready to serve, ladle into individual bowls and top each serving with the scallions.

6 cups broth (beef, chicken, or vegetable)

½ to 1 cup sunflower seeds

2 carrots, thinly sliced in rounds

1 celery rib, thinly sliced

4 scallions with green tops, chopped

VEGETABLE DUMPLING SOUP

Soup:

1 onion, diced

1 T. vegetable oil

4½ cups chicken or vegetable broth

2 cups diced vegetables of choice, such as green beans, peas, carrots, zucchini, broccoli, etc.

1 (15.5 oz.) can great northern or cannellini beans, rinsed and drained

1 tsp. ground mustard

Dumplings:

1 cup Master Biscuit Mix (see page 64)

⅔ cup cornmeal

¼ tsp. oregano

¼ tsp. basil

⅔ cup milk

To make the soup:

In a large, heavy-bottomed soup pot or Dutch oven, sauté the onion in the oil until tender. Add the broth, vegetables, beans, and mustard; stir to combine, bring to a boil, and then cover the pot and simmer for about 8 minutes.

To make the dumplings:

While the soup is simmering, make the dumplings. In a small mixing bowl, combine the biscuit mix, cornmeal, oregano, and basil. Stir in the milk just until blended.

Drop the dumpling dough by tablespoonfuls into the soup. Cover and simmer for 20 minutes without lifting the lid. To check if dumplings are done, insert a toothpick into the middle of one. If it doesn't come out clean, cover the pot again and simmer for another minute or two.

WHITE CHICKEN CHILI

Heat the oil in a large pot over medium heat and then add the onion; cook, stirring occasionally, until tender, about 5 to 10 minutes. Stir in the garlic and then add the chicken, broth, green chilies, cumin, oregano, and cayenne pepper and bring to a boil.

Reduce heat to low and using a potato masher, mash one can of beans until smooth. Add the mashed beans to the pot and stir to combine; add the remaining beans and simmer for 20 to 30 minutes or until the chicken is fully cooked.

Ladle into serving bowls and top with Monterey Jack cheese; also top with optional sour cream and jalapeño peppers and serve immediately.

1 T. vegetable oil

1 onion, chopped

2 cloves garlic, minced

1 lb. boneless skinless chicken breasts (about 4), chopped

2 (14.5 oz.) cans chicken broth

1 (4 oz.) can diced green chilies

2 tsp. ground cumin

2 tsp. oregano

1½ tsp. cayenne pepper

3 (14.5 oz.) cans white kidney or navy beans, rinsed and drained

1 cup shredded Monterey Jack cheese

Sour cream (optional)

Jalapeño peppers (optional)

VEGETABLES AND SIDE DISHES

The recipes in this section will help round out a meal, and some of them can even stand in for a light lunch—add a salad or fresh-baked bread and you're good to go. Some of our favorites include Corn and Green Chili Rice Casserole, Roasted Brussels Sprouts with Hazelnuts and Parmesan, and Zucchini Fritters. And if you've never had the pleasure of eating freshly made noodles, do try the Homemade Egg Noodles. You'll soon be a convert!

BAKED BEETS IN BÉCHAMEL SAUCE

4 medium beets

½ cup water

3 T. butter

1 shallot or small sweet onion, minced

3 T. flour

1 cup milk

¼ cup dry white wine

Salt and pepper to taste

Pinch of nutmeg

Preheat the oven to 425°.

Peel the beets and cut them into ¼-inch-thick slices. Arrange the beets in a large baking dish. Add the water, cover tightly with aluminum foil, and bake for about 45 minutes or until the beets are fork tender.

Meanwhile, melt the butter in a saucepan over medium heat. Add the shallot and sauté until softened, about 3 minutes. Stir in the flour. Slowly whisk in the milk and wine (or substitute wine with ¼ cup broth and a splash of lemon juice), and then bring the mixture to a gentle boil, stirring constantly as it thickens.

Remove the sauce from the heat and add salt and pepper to taste and a pinch of nutmeg. Pour the sauce over the beets in the baking dish and continue to bake, uncovered this time, for about 10 minutes or until the sauce is bubbling and golden brown around the edges.

BARLEY AND PINE NUT PILAF

Preheat the oven to 350°.

Rinse the barley in cold water and drain.

In a large skillet, heat the butter and brown the pine nuts; remove with slotted spoon and set aside.

Sauté the green onions and barley until lightly toasted. Remove the skillet from the heat and stir in the pine nuts, parsley, salt, and pepper. Spoon the mixture into a lightly greased 2-quart casserole dish. Heat broth to boiling and pour over the barley mixture. Stir to blend well.

Bake, uncovered, for 1 hour; check to make sure barley is fully cooked; if not, return to the oven and cook for another 10 minutes or so until done.

1 cup pearl barley

6 T. butter

⅓ cup (2 oz.) pine nuts

1 cup chopped green onions

½ cup fresh chopped parsley (or 2½ T. dried)

¼ tsp. salt

¼ tsp. pepper

3⅓ cups chicken broth

BARLEY CASSEROLE

1 cup pearl barley

5 T. butter, plus more for buttering casserole dish

½ onion, chopped

2½ cups hot water

1 (10.5 oz.) can condensed cream of mushroom soup

1 tsp. salt

½ tsp. pepper

1 clove garlic, minced

Parsley to sprinkle on top (optional)

Rinse the barley in cold water and drain. Butter a 2-quart casserole dish and set aside.

Sauté onion in the butter until softened. Add the barley and sauté until light golden brown. Turn the barley mixture into the prepared casserole dish.

In a mixing bowl, blend the hot water, soup, salt, pepper, and garlic; pour over the barley mixture and mix well.

Cover the casserole and bake for 1 hour; check if barley is cooked and if not, cook for another 5 to 10 minutes and check again.

When ready to serve, top with parsley if desired.

BROCCOLI CASSEROLE

Preheat the oven to 350°. Butter or grease an 8 × 8-inch baking dish.

Steam or boil the broccoli for several minutes or until heated through; drain.

In a mixing bowl, mix the egg, soup, milk, and cheese. Add the broccoli and stir to blend well. Place the mixture in the prepared baking dish.

In a small bowl, mix together the onion rings and melted butter and spread evenly over the top of the broccoli.

Cover the baking dish with a lid (if it has one) or use aluminum foil to cover. Bake for 25 minutes. Remove the lid or foil and continue to bake uncovered for 20 minutes more.

1 (12 oz.) pkg. frozen broccoli, thawed and chopped

1 egg, beaten

1 (10.5 oz.) can condensed cream of mushroom soup

⅓ cup milk

½ cup sharp cheddar cheese

1 cup fried onion rings

2 T. butter, melted

BRUSSELS SPROUTS IN SOUR CREAM SAUCE

1 lb. brussels
sprouts

½ cup chopped
onion

2 T. butter

1 cup sour cream

Salt and pepper to
taste

Smaller is better with brussels sprouts, but if you have larger ones, cut them in half lengthwise, then steam until tender, about 10 minutes; drain well.

Meanwhile, in a large skillet, sauté the onion in the butter until tender, about 3 to 4 minutes. Add the sour cream and heat just until hot but not boiling. (Sour cream will curdle if allowed to boil.) Add the steamed brussels sprouts and mix well. Add salt and pepper to taste and serve immediately.

CAULIFLOWER GRATIN

Clean and cut the cauliflower into florets, all roughly the same size. Steam the cauliflower until tender, about 10 minutes.

While the cauliflower is steaming, preheat the oven to 350°.

Drain the cauliflower and spread it evenly in the bottom of a casserole dish. Spread half of the Gruyère cheese and half of the cheddar cheese over the cauliflower.

In a saucepan, melt 1 tablespoon of the butter over medium heat; add the shallot and sauté until soft. Add the remaining butter to the saucepan and as soon as it melts and begins to sizzle, add the flour, whisking as you add it. Continue whisking for 2 minutes and then slowly pour in the milk while continuing to whisk. Keep whisking and cook until the mixture begins to thicken, about 2 minutes more. Add the wine or additional milk and let cook another minute, still whisking, so the mixture stays thick. Remove from the heat and add salt and pepper to taste.

Pour the sauce evenly over the cauliflower and top with remaining cheese. Sprinkle the panko breadcrumbs evenly over the cheese and bake for 25 minutes; set under the broiler for 1 minute to finish browning the top.

1 head cauliflower

¾ cup shredded Gruyère or Swiss cheese, divided

¼ cup shredded cheddar cheese, divided

2½ T. butter, divided

1 shallot, peeled and minced

3 T. flour

1½ cups milk

1½ T. white wine (or more milk)

Salt and pepper to taste

3 T. panko breadcrumbs

CORN AND GREEN CHILI RICE CASSEROLE

1 cup uncooked long-grain white rice

2 cups water

1 cup cottage cheese

1½ cups frozen corn

1 cup sour cream

2 (4 oz.) cans chopped green chilies

1 cup shredded Mexican-blend cheese

.

Cook rice in water as directed on package.

Meanwhile, preheat the oven to 350°. Using nonstick cooking spray, shortening, or butter, grease the bottom and sides of a 2-quart casserole dish.

In a large bowl, mix all other ingredients except for the Mexican-blend cheese. Add the cooked rice and mix well again. Put the mixture into the prepared dish and then sprinkle the cheese on top.

Bake for 30 to 35 minutes or until the casserole is thoroughly heated and the cheese has melted.

GARLIC PARMESAN BAKED EGGPLANT

Wash eggplant and peel if desired. Slice into discs that are ½-inch thick. Salt both sides of the slices and set them on paper towels to drain for at least 30 minutes. Pat dry.

Preheat the oven to 400°.

Melt the butter in a shallow bowl. In another bowl, mix the dry ingredients.

Dip the eggplant discs in the melted butter first, and then dip into the breadcrumb mixture. Place on a parchment paper–lined baking sheet and bake for 15 minutes; flip the slices over and bake for 7 minutes more.

1 large eggplant (or 2 small eggplants)

6 T. butter, melted

1 cup breadcrumbs

¼ cup grated Parmesan cheese

¼ tsp. smoked paprika

½ tsp. garlic powder

½ tsp. Italian seasoning

HOMEMADE EGG NOODLES

3 egg yolks

1 whole egg

3 T. cold water

1 tsp. salt

2 cups sifted flour

In a large mixing bowl, beat together the egg yolks and whole egg until very light. Add the water, salt, and flour, and beat well again.

Divide the dough into three parts. On a lightly floured, smooth towel (a plain weave towel or flour sacking works best), roll out each piece as thin as possible. Place another towel over the rolled-out dough and let rest until the dough has partially dried.

When ready to cut into noodles, loosely roll up the dough and cut into strips to your desired width. Shake out the strips and allow them to dry further before using or storing. (If you plan on storing the egg noodles, allow them to air dry completely, and then store them in an airtight container at room temperature for up to a month.)

Note: Fresh homemade noodles only need about 2 to 3 minutes to cook, depending on how thick they are. If they are completely dry, they will need a few minutes more cooking time.

MARINATED THREE BEAN SALAD

Rinse and drain the beans and then pour them into a large salad bowl. Add the onion, bell pepper, and celery and mix to combine. Pour in the vinegar, oil, and salt and mix until well blended. Refrigerate overnight to marinate.

Note: This three bean salad doesn't have sweetener of any kind, so if you're watching your sugar intake, it's the perfect recipe. But if you prefer a more traditional three bean salad, here's an alternate dressing recipe:

Mix all alternate recipe ingredients together, pour over the beans and vegetables in place of the vinegar, oil, and salt mixture, stir until well blended, and refrigerate.

1 (14.5 oz.) can cut green beans

1 (15.5 oz.) can garbanzo beans

1 (15.5 oz.) can kidney beans

¼ cup diced onion

¼ cup diced green bell pepper

1 celery rib, diced

½ cup vinegar

¼ cup vegetable oil

1 tsp. salt

Alternate Dressing:

¾ cup sugar

⅔ cup vinegar

⅓ cup vegetable oil

1 tsp. salt

1 tsp. pepper

POTATO CAKE

2 eggs, beaten

1 heaping cup
mashed potatoes

1 cup milk

1½ cups flour

4 tsp. baking powder

1 tsp. salt

1 T. butter, melted

If you're lucky enough to have leftover mashed potatoes, this is a tasty way to use them up.

Preheat the oven to 400°. Grease a large cast-iron skillet or heavy-bottomed ovenproof sauccpan and set aside.

In a large mixing bowl, add the eggs, mashed potatoes, and milk; beat or briskly whisk until smooth. Next, add the flour, baking powder, and salt and mix well again. Add the butter and mix well again. Spoon the potato mixture into the prepared skillet and bake for 25 to 30 minutes or until done and light golden on top.

ROASTED BRUSSELS SPROUTS

Preheat the oven to 425°. Line a baking sheet or jelly roll pan with aluminum foil or a silicone baking mat.

Clean the brussels sprouts, cut off the stems, remove any ragged outer leaves, and cut lengthwise in half. (If the sprouts are very small, you can leave them whole.)

Toss the brussels sprouts with 2 tablespoons of the oil, salt, and pepper; mix well, either directly on the baking sheet or in a large ziplock bag. Spread evenly on the baking sheet and roast for 20 minutes, stirring them halfway through the baking time. Check to see that the brussels sprouts are tender and golden brown. If not, roast for several minutes more.

Drizzle the remaining tablespoon of oil, the balsamic vinegar, and honey over the vegetables and toss to coat evenly. Serve immediately.

1½ lbs. brussels sprouts

3 T. olive oil, divided

1 tsp. salt

½ tsp. pepper

1 T. balsamic vinegar

1 tsp. honey

ROASTED BRUSSELS SPROUTS WITH HAZELNUTS AND PARMESAN

4 T. (½ stick) butter

½ tsp. salt

½ tsp. pepper

1½ lbs. brussels sprouts, trimmed and quartered lengthwise

¼ cup chopped hazelnuts

2 T. shredded Parmesan cheese

Preheat the oven to 450°. Lightly butter or grease a baking dish that is large enough that the brussels sprouts can be laid out in a single layer.

In a small saucepan, melt the butter until bubbling but not yet brown. Remove from heat and stir in the salt and pepper.

Place the brussels sprouts and hazelnuts in the prepared baking dish; drizzle the melted butter over the sprouts and hazelnuts and gently stir to coat.

Roast for 10 to 12 minutes or until the sprouts are tender, stirring occasionally.

Remove from the oven and immediately sprinkle with Parmesan cheese.

ROASTED SWEET POTATOES WITH BACON

Peel the sweet potatoes and cut into a large dice. Preheat the oven to 450°. Lightly grease a 9 × 13-inch baking pan and mix all the ingredients in the prepared baking pan. Bake for 15 minutes; remove the pan from the oven and stir the vegetables. Return the pan to the oven and bake another 15 minutes or until potatoes are done.

2 lbs. sweet potatoes

8 oz. bacon, soft fried and chopped

½ cup diced onion

1½ tsp. chili powder

¾ tsp. salt

½ tsp. ground cinnamon

¼ tsp. cayenne pepper

ROASTED VEGETABLES WITH LIME AND PINE NUTS

2 zucchinis, chunked

½ onion, cut in wedges

1 large tomato, cut in wedges

4 small fingering or red potatoes, cut in half (or left whole if small enough)

8 mushrooms, cut in half (button or cremini)

2 carrots, peeled and chunked

½ cup eggplant, peeled and chunked

½ bell pepper, chunked or cut in wedges

3 T. pine nuts

2 cloves garlic, minced

½ tsp. thyme

1 T. olive oil, more or less

⅛ cup lime juice or to taste

Salt and pepper to taste

Note: I tend to cut my vegetables larger than bite-size because they seem to roast better. Also, you can use more of one vegetable that you especially enjoy and remove other vegetables you don't have or don't like. This is a very forgiving recipe.

Preheat the oven to 400°. Lightly spray a large jelly roll pan with cooking spray or brush the pan with oil.

In a gallon-sized plastic freezer bag, add the vegetables, pine nuts, garlic, and thyme. Drizzle the olive oil over the vegetables (start with 2 teaspoons; add more if needed). Close the top of the bag and gently mix the ingredients so the oil covers the vegetables.

Pour the contents of the bag into the prepared jelly roll pan. Drizzle the lime juice over the vegetables, being careful to coat thoroughly. Add salt and pepper.

Roast for about 15 minutes in the oven. Gently turn the vegetables and continue to roast until the edges begin to brown and the vegetables are crisp-tender, about another 10 to 15 minutes, depending on the size of the chunks. If the vegetables start getting too dark, turn down the oven to 325° and continue to roast just until the vegetables are crisp-tender.

SOUR CREAM SAUCE FOR VEGETABLES

1 part mayonnaise

2 parts sour cream

Pinch of dill weed

Small amount of vinegar or lemon juice

In a small saucepan, mix all ingredients and heat thoroughly over low heat.

Serve over broccoli, cauliflower, brussels sprouts, mixed vegetables, etc.

SPANISH RICE

In a large skillet or pot with a lid, heat the oil and then add the rice. Cook, stirring, until the rice is lightly browned. Turn the heat down to medium-low so the rice doesn't burn. Stir in the onion, green pepper, and celery; sauté until the vegetables are tender, about 3 minutes.

Stir in the tomatoes, water, salt, and chili powder. Bring the mixture to boiling, cover, and simmer for 20 minutes.

When done, fluff the rice with a fork and serve.

2 T. vegetable oil

1 cup uncooked long-grain white rice

¾ cup chopped onion

½ cup chopped green bell pepper

½ cup chopped celery

1 (14.5 to 16 oz.) can stewed tomatoes

1¼ cups water

1½ tsp. salt

1 tsp. chili powder or to taste

SWISS CHARD AND CHICKPEAS

2 T. olive oil

2 shallots, peeled and chopped

5 cloves garlic, minced

2 bunches Swiss chard, center ribs discarded and leaves coarsely chopped

½ cup vegetable broth plus a bit more if needed

1 (15.5 oz.) can chickpeas, rinsed and drained (chickpeas are also called garbanzo beans)

1 T. lemon juice or rice wine vinegar

Salt and pepper to taste

In a large saucepan, heat the oil; add the shallots and sauté for several minutes until the shallots soften. Add the garlic and cook and stir for 1 more minute. Add the Swiss chard and sauté for another few minutes, just until the chard begins to wilt. Pour in the broth and chickpeas and cook, stirring occasionally until the chickpeas are hot. Add the lemon juice and salt and pepper to taste.

VEGETABLE SALAD BOWL

In a large salad bowl, mix the salad ingredients.

In a jar with a tight-fitting lid, add the dressing ingredients and shake vigorously to combine. Pour dressing over the salad and mix to coat all the vegetables; chill thoroughly before serving.

Salad:

2 cups thinly sliced carrots

2 cups diagonally sliced celery

2 cups sliced cucumber (peel, seed, and quarter lengthwise before slicing)

2 cups thinly sliced cauliflower (or 1 cup each sliced cauliflower and broccoli)

1 sweet onion, thinly sliced

1 pint cherry tomatoes, stems removed and cut in half lengthwise

Dressing:

½ cup white vinegar

1 cup olive oil

1½ tsp. salt

¼ tsp. pepper

½ tsp. dry ground mustard

1 clove garlic, minced

½ cup chopped fresh parsley

VICKY'S PILAF

2½ cups chicken or beef broth

4 T. butter

1½ cups uncooked vermicelli noodles, broken into small pieces

1 cup uncooked white rice

Salt and pepper to taste

I had a roommate in college, Vicky, who loved rice pilaf. When it was her turn to cook, we invariably ate pilaf. As a result, I, too, grew fond of the stuff. Rice pilaf is quick and easy, cheap and filling, and this recipe pays homage to those long-ago days.

In a medium saucepan, bring the broth to a boil.

While the broth is heating, melt the butter in a large pot; add the vermicelli noodles and cook, stirring constantly, until the pieces are browned slightly. Add the rice and continue cooking, stirring constantly, for 1 minute more. Pour in the boiling broth, stir, cover the pot, and simmer for 20 to 25 minutes. Add salt and pepper to taste, plus a bit more butter if desired.

ZUCCHINI FRITTERS

Mix zucchini and salt; let stand in strainer over bowl or sink for 15 minutes. Gently squeeze out liquid.

In a bowl, stir together the zucchini, onion, carrot, egg, flour, and pepper.

In a skillet, heat oil over medium-high heat. Drop the zucchini mixture by tablespoonful into pan and fry for 5 minutes on each side or until golden brown. Place the cooked fritters on a paper towel set in an ovenproof pan to drain and place them in a warm oven to keep hot while you fry the entire batch.

Serve these plain, or with ranch dip, blue cheese dressing, or sour cream.

2 medium zucchini, shredded

1 tsp. salt

2 T. finely diced onion

1 carrot, shredded

1 egg, beaten

½ cup flour

Dash of pepper

Vegetable oil or shortening for frying

DESSERTS

Something sweet at the end of a meal just makes everything better. And it doesn't have to be anything elaborate—layering vanilla yogurt, some shaved dark chocolate, and berries is quick and easy, and hits that sweet spot. Or maybe a midmorning break of apple crisp with a hot cup of coffee or tea is more your style. No matter when you choose to eat it, having dessert elevates any meal to something festive and memorable. And it allows us to linger at the dinner table for a bit longer, enjoying conversation and connection with those gathered around.

APPLE CRISP

4 apples, peeled, cored, and sliced

1¼ cups flour

6 T. granulated sugar

6 T. brown sugar

1 tsp. cinnamon

½ cup (1 stick) butter, softened

Preheat the oven to 350°. Butter an 8-inch pie plate or baking dish.

Spread the apples into the prepared pie plate.

Mix the flour, granulated sugar, brown sugar, and cinnamon. Using a pastry cutter or two forks, work in the butter to make a crumbly mixture; spread the mixture over the apples.

Bake, uncovered, for 30 minutes or until the fruit is tender and the topping is a light brown color.

BAKED APPLES WITH WALNUTS AND RAISINS

Preheat the oven to 350°.

Peel the top third of each apple; core. Rub the exposed flesh of the apple with the lemon juice.

In a small mixing bowl, combine the walnuts, raisins, butter, brown sugar, and cinnamon. Place the prepared apples upright into a shallow casserole dish. Stuff the center of the apples with the walnut mixture.

Pour the hot water into the casserole dish, being careful to not pour directly onto the apples. Bake for about 1 hour or until the apples are tender. Remove the baked apples with a slotted spoon and serve them warm.

4 baking apples (such as Granny Smith)

2 T. lemon juice

½ cup finely chopped walnuts

2 T. raisins

2 T. butter, melted and cooled slightly

2 T. brown sugar

1 tsp. cinnamon

1 cup hot water

BERRIES, YOGURT, AND SHAVED CHOCOLATE

2 cups vanilla yogurt, Greek or traditional

2 cups berries (fresh or thawed if frozen), cut into bite-size pieces if necessary

2 dark chocolate bars, shaved (a potato peeler works well)

This is a very simple dessert, and surprisingly elegant, especially if served in goblets.

Gently combine the yogurt and berries. Place a layer of the yogurt mixture into individual serving bowls and sprinkle shaved chocolate on top; repeat the layers, ending with shaved chocolate.

BERRY COULIS

Using a food processor or blender, process berries and lemon juice until smooth; strain with a fine-mesh strainer to remove seeds—this step isn't absolutely necessary, but it makes for a more refined finished product.

Cover and refrigerate; use within one week.

Coulis is excellent mixed with plain yogurt, or used as a topping for pancakes, waffles, panna cotta, cottage cheese, or in a smoothie.

2 cups strawberries or raspberries (fresh or thawed if frozen)

½ tsp. lemon juice

CANNED FRUIT COBBLER

2 cans (about 1 lb. each) cherry or apple pie filling

2 tsp. lemon juice

1½ cups flour

¾ cup sugar

½ cup (1 stick) butter, softened

1 to 2 tsp. cinnamon

½ cup chopped walnuts (optional)

This is a perfect winter recipe because it calls for canned fruit pie filling, and I make a point to add a few cans to my winter pantry. I've also made this recipe using 2 quart-jars of my home-canned blackberries but add 2 tablespoons of cornstarch to the blackberries to help thicken the juice.

Preheat the oven to 400°.

In a large mixing bowl, mix the pie filling with the lemon juice; pour into a 9 × 13-inch baking dish.

In another mixing bowl, add the flour, sugar, butter, and cinnamon. Mix until well blended and crumbly. (Use two forks or your fingers to mix and break into coarse crumbles.) Spread the mixture over the fruit in the baking dish and then add the walnuts if using.

Bake for 20 to 25 minutes or until top is golden brown and bubbly. Let cool for about 5 minutes before serving.

CHOCOLATE TOFFEE

Line a baking sheet with parchment paper and set aside.

In a large pot over medium heat, combine the butter, sugar, vanilla, and salt. Cook, stirring constantly, 12 to 15 minutes or until your thermometer reaches 285°.

Pour the mixture onto the prepared baking sheet and immediately top with the chocolate chips. Let sit for 2 minutes and then spread the melted chocolate over the entire top of the toffee. Spread the nuts over the melted chocolate as evenly as possible so there are no bare spots.

Refrigerate the chocolate toffee until set—at least an hour—and then break the toffee into pieces and serve.

If stored in an airtight container, the toffee will stay good for a week.

1½ cups butter

1½ cups sugar

½ tsp. vanilla

Pinch of salt

2 cups chocolate chips

1 cup sliced almonds, chopped walnuts, or chopped pecans

CRACKLE-TOP MOLASSES COOKIES

4 cups flour

2 T. unsweetened cocoa powder

2 tsp. baking soda

1½ tsp. ground cinnamon

½ tsp. ground cloves

½ tsp. salt

¾ cup butter, softened

1¼ cups granulated sugar, divided

1 cup light molasses

This recipe makes a large batch of cookies—as much as six dozen.

Mix the flour, cocoa, baking soda, cinnamon, cloves, and salt; set aside.

In a large mixing bowl, beat the butter and 1 cup of the sugar with an electric stand mixer until fluffy. Beat in the molasses. With mixer set on low speed, gradually add the flour mixture and beat just until mixed. Divide dough in half; pat each half into a flattened 1-inch-thick round (the shape helps the dough chill quicker). Wrap the rounds in plastic and refrigerate for at least 1 hour to chill.

Preheat the oven to 375°. Lightly grease cookie sheets. Put the remaining ¼ cup sugar in a small bowl.

Use a tablespoon to form dough into 1-inch balls; roll in the sugar and place 1 inch apart on the prepared cookie sheets. Bake for 10 minutes or until evenly browned. Cool on cookie sheet for 1 minute before removing cookies to a rack to cool completely.

CREAM PUFFS

1 cup water

½ cup (1 stick) butter

1 tsp. sugar

¼ tsp. salt

1 cup sifted flour

4 eggs

1 cup heavy cream

¼ cup powdered sugar

½ tsp. vanilla

Preheat the oven to 350°.

In a large saucepan, heat the water, butter, sugar, and salt to a full rolling boil. Add the flour all at once and stir vigorously with a wooden spoon until mixture forms a thick, smooth ball that leaves the sides of the pan clean, about 1 minute. Remove from heat and let the paste cool for a bit so when you add the eggs, they don't inadvertently cook. Add eggs, one at a time, beating well after each addition with the wooden spoon or an electric hand mixer until the paste is shiny and smooth. Shape into puffs of dough and bake for 20 to 30 minutes depending on the size of the cream puffs. When done, they should be puffed, golden, and look a bit dry.

While the cream puffs are baking, make the sweetened whipped cream: In a medium mixing bowl, combine the heavy cream, powdered sugar, and vanilla. Beat the mixture (start with a low speed and increase speed as the mixture thickens so the liquid doesn't splash out of the bowl) until soft peaks form. When the cream puffs have cooled, cut off the tops and spoon the whipped cream into the middle of each cream puff. Replace the tops and serve.

CREEPING CRUST COBBLER

Heat the oven to 350°. Pour the melted butter into an 8 × 8-inch pan.

In a medium mixing bowl, combine the flour, 1 cup of the sugar, the baking powder, and the milk.

In a small saucepan combine fruit and ½ cup of sugar. Adjust the amount of sugar according to the sweetness of the fruit. If the fruit mixture is too juicy, stir in the tapioca or cornstarch and continue to heat until the mixture is slightly thickened.

Pour the fruit mixture over the dough and bake for 30 to 35 minutes or until golden brown.

¼ cup butter, melted

1 cup flour

1½ cups sugar, more or less, divided

1 tsp. baking powder

½ cup milk

2 cups fruit, fresh or canned (peach, blackberry, blueberry, or cherry are good choices)

1 T. instant tapioca or cornstarch (optional)

GINGERBREAD

½ cup boiling water

½ cup shortening

½ cup brown sugar

½ cup light molasses

1 egg, well beaten

1½ cups flour

½ tsp. salt

½ tsp. baking powder

½ tsp. baking soda

¾ tsp. ground ginger

¾ tsp. cinnamon

Another quick and easy recipe, and one of my favorites growing up. We loved eating it slightly warm with a dollop of sweetened whipped cream on top.

Preheat the oven to 350°. Grease and flour an 8 × 8-inch baking pan.

In a mixing bowl, pour boiling water over the shortening. Add brown sugar, molasses, and egg and beat until smooth. Sift the dry ingredients together, add to the mixing bowl, and beat again until smooth. Pour into prepared baking pan and bake for 35 minutes or until done.

GRAHAM CRACKER COOKIES

Preheat the oven to 325°. Grease an 8 × 8-inch baking pan. Cut a piece of waxed paper that fits the bottom of the pan and grease both sides of the paper before laying in the bottom of the greased pan.

Mix all ingredients together and place in the prepared pan; press firmly so it's even and smooth on top.

Bake for 30 minutes. Let stand in the pan for 5 to 10 minutes and then turn the cookies out of the pan. Cut into squares and while still warm, coat the squares in powdered sugar.

2 cups crushed graham crackers

1 (14 oz.) can Eagle Brand sweetened condensed milk

1 cup (6 oz.) chocolate chips

1 tsp. cinnamon

1 tsp. vanilla

Powdered sugar for sprinkling

MIX-IN-THE-PAN CHOCOLATE SNACK CAKE

1⅔ cups flour

1 cup packed brown sugar

¼ cup unsweetened cocoa powder

1 tsp. baking soda

½ tsp. salt

1 cup water

⅓ cup vegetable oil

1 tsp. vinegar

½ tsp. vanilla

This cake is so quick and easy that even a youngster can put it together. When they lived at home, my sons were fond of making this cake when they needed a sweet snack.

Preheat the oven to 350°.

In an ungreased 8 × 8-inch baking dish, use a fork to combine the flour, brown sugar, cocoa powder, baking soda, and salt. When the dry ingredients are blended, add the water, oil, vinegar, and vanilla and continue mixing with the fork until very well blended.

Bake for 35 to 40 minutes or until done.

ORANGE CHIFFON CAKE

While I realize this cake isn't necessarily quick and easy, I'm adding it here because, for years, my mother made this cake when oranges were in season in the fall and winter and it's a delicious memory.

Note: If you don't have cake flour, you can make your own. For 1 cup of cake flour, mix ¾ cup sifted all-purpose flour with 2 T. cornstarch.

Separate the eggs, placing the yolks in one bowl and the whites—along with the extra egg white—in a separate bowl. Cover the bowl that has the egg whites and let them come to room temperature—this should take about 30 minutes.

Preheat the oven to 325° and have ready an ungreased 2-piece tube pan.

In a large mixing bowl, add the flour, all but ¼ cup of the sugar, baking powder, salt, and orange zest. Use a hand mixer to beat until combined. Make a well in the center of the flour mixture and add the egg yolks, oil, orange juice, and vanilla. Beat until smooth, about 1 minute, scraping down the sides of the bowl as needed.

In a separate bowl, with clean beaters, beat the egg whites until foamy. Add the cream of tartar and continue to beat until soft peaks form. Gradually beat in the remaining ¼ cup of sugar and continue to beat until stiff peaks form. With a large rubber spatula or wire whisk, gently fold the egg whites into the batter, a bit at a time, just until blended, being careful not to deflate the batter.

Pour the cake batter into the tube pan and bake for 55 to 60 minutes, or until a toothpick or wooden skewer inserted into the center of the cake comes out clean. Remove from the oven and immediately invert the tube pan and place on

6 large eggs

1 egg white

2¼ cups sifted cake flour

1½ cups caster (superfine) sugar, divided

1 T. baking powder

½ tsp. salt

2 T. grated orange zest (use the peel only, as the white pith is bitter)

½ cup vegetable oil

¾ cup freshly squeezed orange juice

1 tsp. vanilla

½ tsp. cream of tartar

Powdered sugar (optional)

Sweetened whipped cream (optional)

Fresh fruit (optional)

a bottle or flat surface so it is suspended over the counter. Let the cake cool completely before removing from the pan. To remove, carefully run a long metal spatula or broad knife around the inside of the tube pan and center core. Invert the cake onto a greased wire rack.

Right before serving, dust the top of the cake with powdered sugar or serve with sweetened whipped cream and fresh fruit if desired. The cake can sit at room temperature but will last longer if refrigerated.

POUND CAKE

Note: If you don't have cake flour, you can make your own. For 1 cup of cake flour, mix ¾ cup sifted all-purpose flour with 2 T. cornstarch.

Preheat the oven to 325°. Lightly grease a 9 × 5-inch loaf pan. Line the bottom and ends with parchment paper, allowing the ends to hang over for easy removal of the cake after baking.

In a medium bowl, whisk together the regular flour, cake flour, baking powder, and salt.

In the bowl of a stand mixer, cream the butter and sugar on medium-low speed until light and fluffy, about 4 to 5 minutes. Add the eggs and egg yolks one at a time, until mixed well. Scrape sides of the bowl as needed. Add the vanilla and mix again until well combined. Turn the speed to medium-high and continue beating for 2 minutes.

Beginning and ending with the flour mixture, alternately add the flour mixture and the milk and continue mixing until batter is well blended and smooth. Pour the batter into the prepared loaf pan.

Bake for 50 to 60 minutes; check after 50 minutes to see if the cake is done. The cake is done when it springs back after gently pressing the top. Also, if the cake looks to be browning too quickly, loosely cover the top with aluminum foil and continue baking.

Remove the cake from the oven and let it cool in the pan for 10 minutes before pulling the loaf from the loaf pan and cooling completely on a rack.

1 cup flour, spooned into the measuring cup with a light touch and leveled

1 cup cake flour, spooned and leveled

1 tsp. baking powder

½ tsp. salt

1 cup butter, softened to room temperature

1 cup granulated sugar

2 large eggs, room temperature

4 egg yolks, room temperature

1 tsp. vanilla

½ cup milk, room temperature

SPICE CAKE

½ cup shortening

1 cup sugar

2 eggs

⅓ cup light molasses

2½ cups flour

¼ tsp. salt

2½ tsp. baking powder

¾ tsp. cloves

¾ tsp. allspice

¾ cup milk

Preheat the oven to 350°. Grease two 9-inch cake pans and line the bottoms with parchment or waxed paper.

In a large bowl or the bowl of a stand mixer, thoroughly cream together the shortening and sugar. Add eggs, one at a time, and beat after each addition. Beat in the molasses.

In another bowl, sift together the flour, salt, baking powder, cloves, and allspice. Add the dry ingredients, a bit at a time, and alternately add in the milk, beating after each addition. Pour the batter equally between the two pans and bake for 30 to 35 minutes or until the cake springs back when lightly pressed or a toothpick inserted in the middle comes out clean.

SWEDISH GINGER COOKIES

This is another longstanding family recipe, and the flavor lends itself to wintertime. But that didn't stop our family from making these cookies anytime the mood struck us. They're just that good! Also, this recipe makes 6 to 7 dozen cookies, so it's a perfect choice for a party or potluck.

In a large mixing bowl, add the butter, brown sugar, egg, molasses, and evaporated milk; mix thoroughly.

In another large bowl, add the flour, baking soda, ginger, cinnamon, cloves, allspice, and salt and blend until thoroughly mixed. Add these dry ingredients into the molasses mixture, stirring until thoroughly mixed. Cover the bowl and refrigerate the dough for at least 2 hours to chill.

When ready to bake, preheat the oven to 375°. Lightly grease a cookie sheet.

Roll out a portion of the dough to ⅛ to ¼-inch thick, using as little flour as possible to keep dough from sticking. Cut into desired shapes and place 1 inch apart on the prepared cookie sheet. Bake for 8 to 10 minutes or until done.

When the cookies have cooled, frost them with a thin powdered sugar icing or glaze.

½ cup butter, softened

1 cup packed brown sugar

1 large egg

1 cup molasses

½ cup evaporated milk (or heavy cream)

5 cups sifted flour

1 tsp. baking soda

1 tsp. ginger

1 tsp. cinnamon

½ tsp. ground cloves

½ tsp. allspice

½ tsp. salt

RECIPE INDEX

RESOURCES

MUST-HAVE BOOKS

The Homestead Canning Cookbook by Georgia Varozza. Everything you ever wanted to know about canning can be found in this book along with plenty of recipes to get you up and running. Including home-canned jars of food in your pantry is food confidence at its best.

The Homestead Sourdough Cookbook by Georgia Varozza. For beginners and experienced sourdough bakers alike. I take beginners step-by-step through the process of making their first loaf of sourdough bread, but with more than a hundred recipes, you won't run out of inspiration. Provides information on finding the tools and supplies you need plus making or sourcing your own quality starter.

USEFUL ONLINE STORES

Amazon: **amazon.com** Amazon has about anything you could think of, and prices are always competitive. Some items I regularly buy from Amazon are organic rice and Bob's Red Mill products.

Augason Farms: **augasonfarms.com** They sell dehydrated and freeze-dried foods of all kinds that come in #10 cans. Augason Farms products are available at grocery stores pretty much everywhere, including Walmart, and their prices can't be beat.

Azure Standard: **azurestandard.com** Azure Standard is a family-owned business that has grown to encompass most of the United States. They deliver per a set schedule all over the country. Azure offers bulk food items including organic food (fresh, canned, frozen, and dehydrated), farm equipment and livestock feed, home goods, books, and so much more. It's worth checking them out.

Berkey Water Filter Systems: **myberkey.com** A one-stop (online) shop for everything you could possibly need for a water filtration system.

Bob's Red Mill: **bobsredmill.com** Bob's Red Mill no longer sells to customers directly from their online store. Instead, you'll find their products just about everywhere. But the website is still active so you can peruse their offerings.

Central Milling: **centralmilling.com** Central Milling has been in business for more than 150 years, and they're still going strong today. They sell grains and flour among other items. Their selection is large, and their quality is excellent.

Cottage Craftworks: **cottagecraftworks.com** This online store has an abundance of nonelectric tools and appliances. Over the years, I have purchased many items that have helped me become more self-reliant and I've never been disappointed. Check them out—you'll be glad you did.

Hoosier Hill Farm: **hoosierhillfarm.com** Hoosier Hill offers dehydrated dairy products as well as many pantry essentials, baking staples, special diet, and so much more.

King Arthur Baking Company: **kingarthurbaking.com** This is a great website that offers everything you need for baking.

Lehman's Hardware: **lehmans.com** Located in Kidron, Ohio, Lehman's has been in business for years and caters to the Amish. If you ever go to their store, you'll be transported to another time with their large selection of non-electric and old-fashioned items for sale. Thankfully, for those of us who can't get to Ohio, their website sells everything in stock.

Local farmers markets: Farmers markets are great for buying bulk produce in season, so if you have plans to, say, can tomato sauce, a farmers market will net you high-quality, fresh tomatoes.

Montana Milling: **montanamilling.com** Montana Milling produces and sells a wide variety of grains and flour. I am a longtime customer, and the quality is always top notch.

Mountain Rose Herbs: **mountainroseherbs.com** Bulk herbs, spices, teas, oils, and so much more. I shop here for my homemade body oils, soap making, decorative jars, and lots more.

My Patriot Supply: **mypatriotsupply.com** Water filtration systems, emergency food, bulk food, open pollinated seeds.

Sprout People: **sproutpeople.org** I've purchased from Sprout People many times and I'm always pleased with the quality of the seeds. They also offer sprout and microgreens kits and supplies.

W.T. Kirkman Lanterns: **lanternnet.com** I love this online store! They carry truly remarkable oil lamps.

ABOUT THE AUTHOR

Georgia Varozza, author of *The Homestead Canning Cookbook* and *The Homestead Sourdough Cookbook*, enjoys teaching people how to prepare and preserve healthy foods, live simply, practice self-reliance, and get the most from what they have. She is a writer and editor and lives in the Pacific Northwest.

ALSO BY GEORGIA VAROZZA...

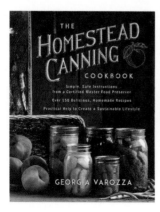

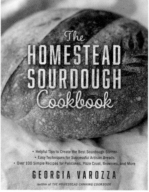

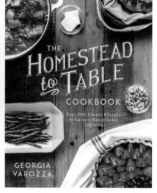